The Gyrlfriend Code™ Volume 1

A collection of 14 unique voices, perspectives and codes to help transform the way we see ourselves, connect, support, and uplift our gyrlfriends

A Gyrlfriend Collective Publication

Gyrlfriend Collective Co-Founders

info@gyrlfriendcollective.com

Ordering Information:

Quantity Sales: Special discounts are available on quantity purchases by organizations, associations, and nonprofits. For details, contact the publisher at the address above.

Designed & Published by Gyrlfriend Collective LLC

This book is intended to be used with accompanying journal as a conversation starter. It is an opportunity to reflect on the relationships shared amongst gyrlfriends. It aims to impart empathy, invigorate friendships and illuminate our best selves as women. This book is not intended to provide financial, emotional health or legal advice. Please seek appropriate counsel for financial, emotional health or legal matters.

A Message from the Visionary Authors

What is The Gyrlfriend Code?

A code is a system of principles or rules. The Gyrlfriend Code™ is a collection of unspoken principles we use to govern ourselves, expectations and the relationships we ultimately have with our gyrlfriends. Identifying and understanding varying perspectives on Gyrlfriend Code, even if it is not one that you subscribe to, helps strengthen our ability to maintain long lasting relationships.

What started off as a way to engage with other women on a social level, has transformed into a flourishing platform offering opportunities for women to collectively share experiences and advice that has enriched their lives and the relationships shared with their gyrlfriends.

We put effort into every other relationship we have: with our families, spouses, even the relationships we have at work. Although we have the potential to have the longest relationship with our gyrlfriends, this has consistently been the relationship we are quickest to abandon. This is the rationale behind the "y" in the spelling of our organization's name and growing movement.

The Gyrlfriend Collective movement and The Gyrlfriend Code™ represent the sum total of our voices ready to change the narrative on gyrlfriend relationships.

The Gyrlfriend Collective Co-Founders

Maureen Carnakie-Baker
Dr. Marquita Smith Blades
Cynthia A. Fontan

Special Dedication

For my brother Dwayne, who was not a "gyrlfriend", but was my first friend. This is for you.
~ **Dr. Marquita S. Blades**~

For infusing Goodness, Joy, and Wisdom into my everyday life, I dedicate this book to my Gyrlfriends and Goddesses-past, present and future. I love you.
~ **Laura Rudacille**~

In loving memory of my Mom, who made me the woman I am today. I miss you so much!
~**Nancy Mathieu**~

In loving memory of my beautiful Gyrlfriend Sonja Goldson-Trotman, you are my light, my rock, my human diary. You will always have a special place in my heart!
~**Ethlyn "Liz" Lewis**~

For my sisters Sonia, Evelyn and Melissa. We are sisters by blood and gyrlfriends by choice. XOXO!
~**Cynthia A. Fontan**~

For my mom whom I love dearly, my sisters Monya and Michele who will always have my back, and daughters Ciara, Giovanni and Kayla. I'm proud to be your mother.
~**Dawn Ortiz**~

This book is dedicated to my family, friends, Sorors and colleagues.
~**Dr. Melissa Noland Chester**~

For my mom, whose love and sacrifices has shaped me into the woman I am. This is also a special dedication to my late sister, Deborah, my first gyrlfriend and my personal "secret keeper."
I carry you with me in all that I do. I love you.
~Maureen Carnakie-Baker~

To all that rooted for my rise, thank you!
The mature women who raised me; Mom, Aunt Angela and Grandma, and my gyrlfriends who are not my blood but are family made, you know who you are.
~Dr. Tricialand Hilliard~

For my gyrlfriend and Soror Tomeka Wright.
I miss you more than words can express.
~Teresa Suber Goodman~

I would like to dedicate this book to Kitara Bingham, a dedicated mother, daughter, author and the realest of gyrlfriends you could ever have. We became instant friends, we totally understood each other's Aquarius Crazy, and laughed through our growth.
I truly miss you.
~E Che'meen Johnson~

Dedicating my chapter in loving memory to Latoya Ritter.
~Ashley Little~

My chapter is dedicated to my sisters by blood: Arica, Alicia, Nikki, and Jessica; and, my sisters by fire: Natalie, Quita, and Sharonda. There is no greater gift than true friends.
~Ariel Dixon~

Table Of Codes

1. The Reality Code
   Gyrlfriend, It's Not About You...........11
2. The Connection Code
   Stronger Together........................23
3. The Secrecy Code
   Between You and I.......................37
4. The Partnership Code
   I Am My Gyrlfriend's Keeper.............47
5. The Honesty Code
   Not Without My MasKara................61
6. The Resilience Code
   From Breaking Point to Turning Point...75
7. The Success Code
   Gyrlfriends' Solution To Success.........83
8. The Financial Code
   Counting Her Coins.....................103
9. The Maturity Code
   The Grown Gyrlfriend...................117
10. The Adaptation Code
    From The Inside Looking Out...........135
11. The Hierarchy Code
    There are Levels to Gyrlfriendship......145
12. The Seasonal Code
    Seasons of Friendship...................157
13. The Self-Reflection Code
    Jealous Much?..........................165
14. The Labeling Code
    The Tragedy of the Instant Bestie........171

~Meet The Authors~..............................187

Dr. Marquita S. Blades

Visionary Author & Gyrlfriend Collective Co-Founder

Dr. Blades helps us examine our experiences, understanding that many of the things that happen to us are not a reflection of who we are or what we've done. People hypothesize about the reasons they experience things, including setbacks in gyrlfriend relationships. Sometimes things happen, and they genuinely have nothing to do with you.

The Reality Code
Gyrlfriend, It's NOT about YOU!

You just lost one

After not speaking to a good friend for years, I was happy that we had finally reconnected. She'd found me on Facebook, or I her, and we made plans to meet for lunch. I was on pins and needles! (For those who aren't from the South, this means I was really excited.) I could not wait to catch her up on everything that happened during the time that I'd allowed our friendship to lapse. I was itching (this also means excited) to hear about her life as well. The morning of, however, she messaged me saying that she needed to reschedule, so we did.

The time had come again for my friend and me to meet. I was ready. I even remembered some things I needed to tell her that I had not thought about the first time. This time, I even selected my outfit in advance. This lunch date was long overdue. This time, I called the night before to confirm. She did not answer, so I left a message. To me, this was no big deal, but the next morning, she messaged me via FB Messenger and cancelled again. This time, her kid had a school function that she had to attend. Now this I found odd. Most school events are planned well in advance, so it seemed as if she should have known about this when I proposed the new date of our meeting. Although I had the suspicion that this meeting would never really happen, I did reach out a couple more times and received no response.

It became apparent to me that she had no intention of rekindling our friendship. Maybe she did in the beginning but decided later to leave well enough alone, to let sleeping dogs lie, as we say. Maybe she'd spoken to some of her other friends, and they had reminded her that I'd basically just dropped off of the face of the earth with no explanation. *What type of friend would do that?* Clearly, I had torn my draws (those are panties) with her, and there was no sewing or patching them up. Whatever the reason, I knew that what we once had would no longer be, and I was okay with that.

This situation is just one example of friendships gone awry due to nothing more than a lack of communication on my part. I am the first to admit that I am not the most communicative person. I don't like aimlessly talking on the phone, and I don't really care for hanging out very often. I don't need a lot of attention. By all definitions, I am an introvert, and I enjoy being by myself most of the time. This does not mean I don't love my friends, but I certainly don't need to be in constant contact with them in order to feel close to them. One thing's for sure, I could never be accused of wearing out my welcome.

How many friendships end this way? With one friend pulling a disappearing act, leaving the other to wonder what they may have said or done to drive them away? The greater question is, though, why do we tend to think that we are such a factor in other people's decisions or actions? Why do we look inward when other people behave in an unexpected way? It's **not** about *you*, Gyrlfriend!

Rarely, if ever, is it about *you*! I know that we like to believe that we are special, especially in the eyes of our gyrlfriends. To a degree, we are, but in the grand scheme of things, we are not as special as we build ourselves up to believe. We are not so special that our feelings can dictate the actions of our gyrlfriends when they are making decisions about how and when they will interact with us. Don't believe I'm telling the truth? Well, just think about all the advice you've given to your gyrlfriends that they did not follow! Still feel so special? Consider, if you will, that your gyrlfriends' behavior may have absolutely nothing to do with you!

So, what could be more important than one's gyrlfriends?

I'll tell you what. It's survival. So many women are functioning in survival mode—doing just enough to make it through each day. Many women are fighting silent battles that make it difficult and sometimes impossible to show up for what most would consider the simple things; the things that most women find relaxing or fun: spa days, movie nights, or a night out with the gyrls for drinks. For some women, the thought of a gyrl's night out is exhausting, or frightening, even, considering the loads of personal issues that they are carrying on a daily basis. While many are able to carry these loads and still maintain their friendships, others are either incapable of or unwilling to do the same.

What are these so-called silent battles? There are several including insecurities, abusive relationships, mental illness, chronic illness, marital problems, and financial difficulties just to name a few. I can only speak from experience, so I'll share with you the silent battles that I have personally fought and how they impacted my relationships with my gyrlfriends.

The first is when I became involved with an abusive narcissist. Yes, I was in an abusive relationship! When I first started dating him, the signs went right over my head. Looking back, it is so obvious to me that his primary motive was controlling me and manipulating my family and friends.

It started with him asking me not to answer my friends' calls when we were together. Under normal circumstances, I would have never complied with such a request; however, he worked out of state and was gone 20 out 30/31 days each month. In this case, we didn't have much time together, so I thought his request made sense, and I went along with it. On the rare occasions that I would answer a friend's call anyway—let's say, for instance, he was pumping gas or was already on his phone—he'd get mad and an argument would ensue. (It should be noted that I had never even had arguments in my previous adult relationships. It's just not something that I do, but here I was doing it.) Because I am not an argument type of person, over time, it just became easier to not answer the phone when he was around. I missed a lot of calls from a lot of friends, and I never shared with them why I was not picking up when they called. My gyrlfriends did not know that the missed calls were not about them but were about my survival in a toxic relationship. It just got to the point where I needed to keep the peace. I figured I'd have time to patch up my relationships with my gyrlfriends later.

I knew that I'd allowed this relationship to get too far gone when my hairstylist, who is also one of my best friends, had to pay me a visit at work! He came to the school where I was teaching without calling me because for the first time in our 14-year relationship, I had not been coming to my weekly hair appointments, nor had I been calling him to say I wasn't coming or to reschedule. He knew something was wrong because this behavior was completely out of character for me, his friend. He never asked to see me while he was at my school; he simply left a note that said, "I don't know what is going on, but I hope this helps." The note included $200.00 in cash. Boy, did he know me! Not only was this narcissist making it difficult for me to get my hair done without there being an on-going argument about it (he wanted me to switch to a female hairstylist who was also his cousin—which I refused to do), but I was so strapped for money because I was going through foreclosure and also trying to pay a past due balance to my university so I could re-enter and complete my doctoral program.

My friend, although not a gyrl in this case, knew that it was not about him! He knew me well enough to know that there must have been something else going on to cause me to behave this way. He immediately removed emotion from the situation and thought about it logically, and he was 100 percent correct in his thinking. Well ultimately, his visit and monetary gift was the straw that broke the narcissist's back and led to the physical assault that ended our relationship. There were some gyrlfriends that I did not talk to during this time, and when I looped back around to try to tell them what I'd been through, they were no longer there. They thought it was about them.

Speaking again from experience, there are periods of time when I truly can't talk to anyone other than my mother or my husband. When I say *can't*, I mean *can't*, as in I don't have enough energy, I do not have the mental capacity, or a combination of the two. This is usually when I am experiencing a flare up from lupus, an autoimmune disease that I was diagnosed with about ten years ago. During these extremely painful periods, the only thing that I can truly focus on is relieving the pain and regaining my strength. Because these flare ups are so intense in nature, I typically lose most, if not all, independence and require a high level of assistance and care. I don't have anything to give to another person—not even a decent conversation. Hell, I don't have anything to give to myself! Answering the phone is the last thing I want to do when I'm not well. And the other last thing I want to do is bring someone else down with me. It's just easier for me not to call or answer calls, but it's never about my gyrlfriends.

Earlier this year, I spent nine days in the hospital due to lupus complications and a septic bacterial infection. I did not call any of my gyrlfriends to tell them I'd been admitted. They would have wanted to see me, and I didn't have the desire to be seen. When you isolate yourself in this way, you know that you are playing roulette with your relationships, but in the moment, you take the chance and bet on yourself. You bet on the fact that your friends will still be there when you emerge from the trials. *Gyrlfriends, it's not about you!*

I've also faced financial hardships that kept me from communicating with my gyrlfriends. When I decided to re-enroll in my doctoral program, I was significantly underemployed, making about 15k less than I'd previously made, my foreclosure was still pending, and I'd just broken up with the narcissist. My lupus was completely out of control, and I could barely take care of myself physically or financially. I wound up taking a one-bedroom apartment in my hometown so that my mother could move in and become my full-time caregiver. During this time, I had to sacrifice a lot of the things that I'd previously enjoyed about life. This included some of my gyrlfriends. I simply could not afford the relationships. Living an hour from the city made it difficult to see them for dinner for multiple reasons:

17

1. I didn't have enough money for any extras (meals, gas, parking, or tips)

2. The drive would exacerbate the physical pain that I felt daily

3. I'd gained so much weight from the medication that I barely had any clothes that fit and I didn't feel as if the ones I could fit into looked good on me (I already told y'all I was broke, so buying anything new was not even an option)

4. If, by chance, I did have some extra money, was not in pain, and could find something to wear that I felt somewhat confident in, there would be the challenges that I encountered while I was out—not being able to open a restaurant door because my muscles were too weak, not being able to touch a fork because cold metal causes my fingers to turn purple and go numb, having to explain yet again to my gyrlfriends what lupus is, and also having to hear about how I "don't look sick" or that "I looked good thick."

5. Let's just say again that I was somehow able to make it out. The fatigue that would follow often left me unable to function for the next one to three days. This meant no lesson plans would be written, no research for my dissertation would be conducted, and I might possibly have to miss a day of work (and consequently, a day of my already meager pay—and I'd be left with what we call a *lil'*

pissy check), because being as sick as I was, I had long since exhausted my bank of sick days.

Oh, *hunty*, this was never about my gyrlfriends. I was literally just doing the best I could to survive and make it another day so that one day, I *could* be the gyrlfriend I'd been in the past. The one that could be called for a last-minute road trip. The one who listened and gave sound relationship advice. The one who was fun to be around. The confident, dependable gyrlfriend who had her stuff together. For another gyrl, the reasons for not keeping up with her gyrlfriends may be completely different but can lead to the very same results: being seen as a fly-by-night, insincere, fair-weather friend, when in fact, she is quite the opposite.

You see, although I made it well-known that I was battling lupus, I did not take it personally when gyrlfriends did not check on me. I did not take it personally when gyrlfriends did not take the time to try to understand my illness or offer me any assistance. I never once thought it was about *me*. I figured they must have had something going on that needed their attention more than I did and that was perfectly fine with me. I got it! In my mind, if we have ever been friends and we have not had any disagreements, then we are still friends—even if we have not spoken in years.

I actually have a great group of friends for which this is the case. We see each other only for special occasions—graduations, baby showers, weddings, and unfortunately, funerals too. None of us ever assume that anything is wrong simply because we have not spoken. In fact, I do believe that I may be the only one who is truly out of the loop—I think they meet for monthly dinners. They don't ask me to come, and I don't ask them why they don't ask me to come. We all understand that it is not about any of us, but more about life and the different paths each of ours has taken. We don't expect to still be doing the exact same things the exact same ways that we did them in high school and college. It just isn't realistic or practical. But we do expect to show up for each when it really matters, and that is what we continue to do.

Consider This – My Advice to all Gyrlfriends

There comes a point in life when friendships should be able to sustain themselves without constant nurturing. Sure, I understand that whole concept of having to be a friend in order to have a friend, and I believe it has merit. However, I will also admit that I don't always play by the rules, and in spite of this, I still expect to have solid friendships.

Most women are not okay with avoiding or ignoring their friends. If this is the case, look deeper. There may be something going on that is preventing your gyrlfriend from being the friend she once was. Don't just assume that it has anything to do with you. You're a woman for Pete's Sake; you have unmatched intuition. If something were truly "off" in your relationship, you'd definitely know it. (I am speaking strictly about situations in which gyrlfriends have not had a "falling out" as we call it where I'm from. If you know that you have done something shady, then this does not apply to you. In the event that you and your gyrl have gotten into it, it **IS** about you, gyrlfriend! If this is you, get somewhere and sit down until that gyrl is ready to talk to you again!)

Finally, let's get over ourselves. Let's stop giving ourselves so much credit and thinking that all actions revolve around us. Let's be mindful that the gyrl we know and love may be a representative at times and that her choice to keep her struggles hidden is not a reflection on us or our worth as a gyrlfriend. Let's give our gyrlfriends space as needed and allow them to come back to us when and if they are ready. Let's also understand that our gyrlfriends may no longer want to be friends, and we can let her go without questioning ourselves and what we could have done differently. Let us all just remember that it may not be about us, gyrlfriends!

Laura Rudacille

Co-Author

Laura's goal is to help women learn to stand shoulder to shoulder, connected. We must learn to lean on one another and uplift each other. Being connected and supportive of one another is vital to womanhood. It strengthens us collectively. The sum total is always greater than the individual.

The Connection Code
Stronger Together

"Grab your floatie, noodle, inner tube, inflatable unicorn, and get in here!" My heart swells as I absorb the sight of the vast sea of womanhood. Colorful spandex amplifies beauty in all shapes and sizes. Fierce, triumphant, resilient, wisdom-rich, well-seasoned women floating it out in connected unity. Stronger Together, they beckon others to join them in the water knowing fine-tuned friendships fortify. This vision of fullness and encouragement wasn't where my image of female friendships began.

My early splashes in the kiddie pool offered spunky 'wanna play' Snoopy-styled associations. Age and time offered relationships with layered complexity. I dove into the deep end, arms and legs in constant motion, as I tried to keep my head above water. On occasion, I'd slip beneath the surface and come up sputtering, surprised and hurt as I realized the 'Lucys' sharing the water had paddled away. Exposed and vulnerable, I'd return to a depth where my toes could touch.

Shallow water friendships often led me to the wrong people, the wrong places, and the wrong behaviors. My self-inflicted margin of protection resulted in a lack of expectation and delivered exactly what I exuded. Cumulative impacts had me climbing from the water to seek solid ground, stability, and shade. I protected myself by limiting my roads, walking only where the path was clearly marked and the destination was predetermined. I formed opinions, guidelines for security, and erected walls of protection. Years zipped past, and my cautious route proved to be an autopilot highway to loneliness. My guarded heart, though safe, prevented the enriching goodness of connected womanhood from finding me.

I've learned many lessons on my pathway of **becoming**. The most important is the road to womanhood isn't meant to be traveled alone. Be on the lookout for good company on the road. We are Stronger Together. Connection with women who enrich and encourage is vital. Good company, the women you're meant to partner with, transcends beyond zip code, school, workplace, and dare I say it, bloodline. Women who'll champion healing and promote your becoming process beyond self-imposed belief or limitation. Women who'll provide strength when you're wobbly, inspire you to stand, and remain shoulder to shoulder with you until you're ready to move forward. Women whose impact is felt long after the encounter and whose enrichment tangles with and reinforces your thoughts and actions beyond the moment. Transformation, growth, and unity, leading to goodness beyond measure... challenging perhaps, but not impossible.

Our personal fullness rises as we release expectation and become expectant, as we discover healing through trust and welcome the return to self. I've come to understand I can't outsmart my personal healing. My first stone of protection was placed when I was a child, and I've positioned decades of well-meaning defensive barriers. Deconstruction cultivates openness and invites empowering strength in connection. Getting "healthy" takes effort and time, but as our stumbling blocks become stepping stones, the wave of healing isn't a gentle whisper but a torrent rush of collaboration and kinship.

I began by inviting me, all of me, to the truth table and embraced who I am in this moment. And then, I reminded myself whose I am always. Armed with truths and wisdoms learned on my road of **becoming**, I was ready to face my first stone.

Dear twelve-year-old Laura,

This evening, huddled on a dark staircase during a sleepover, you'll learn about the ugly twists of humanity from children. Their giggling whispers will move like a persistent breeze through tall grass. The undulating waves of destruction will stall parts of your free spirit, and your definition of friendship will be altered. From this moment, the depth of the water you're willing to wade into becomes shallow. Your fearlessness and willing cannonball plunge into the deep end is set aside. You'll become a master of the brave face, and the muscle you'll train and flex is control.

The gossip drifting across the quiet of the bedroom will prove to be as impacting as the content of their chatter, your father's infidelity. You'll feel abandoned and discardable, wondering why friends find amusement in sharing hurtful hearsay. Confidence eroded in perceived rejection, you'll question what's in you that caused compassion and love to switch off? All I can tell you is the road ahead will be long. There will be countless peaks and valleys. There will be brilliant storms and beautiful rainbows. Let me assure you, I'll meet you again sooner than you expect. Hang in there, you are **becoming**.

~ Love, You today, Me

Fractured trust made me wary of relationships in any form. Self-sufficiency became my favorite justification. Guarding my heart from blindside betrayal, I convinced myself alone didn't equal lonely and added boulders to fortify my walls. A mad-skilled mason, my fortress was reinforced and virtually impenetrable, keeping at bay potential connections good and bad as I remained safely inside. My self-sufficiency would prove to be a profound spirit killer.

Opportunities for connection were lost in my desire to control. As friendships became available, I only exposed a fraction of myself. When invitations were extended, I responded, "I couldn't possibly," and filled in an excuse. I still didn't know what made me discardable. Snoopy relationships eluded me, but I seemed to collect Lucys, and the ball was continually being pulled away just as I was set to kick. I poured myself into my work and home life and ticked off society's prerequisites of achievement and benchmarked adulthood. I tried on *costumes,* hurting myself and others in the process. Reckless behavior compromised my body and heart, and apologies would fail to erase all the impacts. My voice grew quiet. I lost myself in fragments . . . in miniscule shifts of values. A twisted penance for all I was not. I discovered real life happily-ever-after was a full-time job which required sanity checks and, on occasion, fresh cocktails. The epidemic of hurt woven through the human condition flashed like neon billboards lining my road. I became the Queen of Fine. I bought shoes that didn't fit and wore them despite the pain and blisters. Our becoming is messy business.

I began to share the road with the broken—like recognizes like. Drawn together, offering the little we felt secure and comfortable sharing. My shadow sisters, Contortion and Compromise, joined the ride, and additional pieces of who I was were set aside, thwarting the process of becoming who I was designed to be. My internal dialog was deafening, and lost inside, my broken twelve-year-old sobbed. I had yet to understand growth is as unrelenting as flowing water. Thankfully, God leads even when we cannot see.

A clever shift occurred, and I found myself in the salon industry. The appointment-driven business validated my worthiness and provided an array of multifaceted souls enduring wide-ranging circumstances as they navigated every season of life. Unscripted, candid connection over sudsy water and penetrating pigment would shift my heart with subtle, safe healing. Persistent droplets of goodness loosened the mortar linking my protective walls and delivered powerful, life giving water . . . and I was so thirsty. (Come to the well, and let your bucket sink . . . (John 4:4-26)) My passport to discovery existed in the gift of listening. "I felt it shelter to speak with you." (Emily Dickinson)

"I'm going to take my hair off now," a grandmother and Holocaust survivor said as she dropped her wig into her lap. "Let them look," the battered woman said defiantly as she displayed her blooming black eye. I comforted a teary mother through her child's first haircut, then a few years later, shaved her head in preparation for chemotherapy. I earned my PhD in living life as one appointment at a time the capacity and strength to overcome, seek, persist, and release in amazing ways was revealed. This new dimension of depth and candor knocked a huge hole in my understanding of female relationships and provided insight outside of family situations and zip code friendships. Healing was hiding in plain sight under the hood dryer. Goddesses, I'd come to call them; well-seasoned, fiercely self-assured women in their seventies and eighties adorned with plastic rollers and gentle smiles offered profound wisdom and clarity. Their insight provided and an opportunity for forgiveness. I had the capability to let go of my ideas, broad stroke definitions, limited trust, and could choose to be vulnerable. I fell in love with the hopeful possibility that I too would become as feisty, unapologetic, seasoned, and secure as they.

We are Stronger Together. The road of my becoming is not meant to be traveled alone. Weary of seeking security, I dipped a toe in and tested the water attending dinner dates and social outings but was quick to proclaim, "My friend card is full." My inner child motioned me to take her hand. "Sit with me and stay safe." I listened and revisited the shallow end. Comfortable among the broken, I settled in for no depth or 'give you a kidney' relationships. Once again, God knew what he was doing.

"You must be who you're looking for," my eighty-year-old Goddess Isabella said. "Show me who your friends are, and I'll show you what you are." How "all in" would I dare to wade to discover the prize of connection and strength offered in the community of other women? Time for an intentional shift . . . Be who I'm looking for . . . My shadow sisters Contortion and Compromise grew up and became Connection and Collaboration.

Taking a page from the fearless girl I'd been once upon a time, I rented a cabin in Woodstock, NY for a writer's conference. I attended sessions and workshops, choosing any seat available. An energetic group of women invited me to join them for dinner. "I couldn't possibly" flew from my lips and slammed my protective gate down, sealing my fortress. The Cha-Cha of familiar had me re-mortaring my walls. Guarding my heart, limiting my ability to receive and embrace enriching connections. Isolated by my own actions, I sat alone in my car as disappointment washed over me in a flood of tears. If I never trusted, I'd never grow.

I climbed from the car and walked into the patio bar and ordered dinner. I lingered over my meal and captured my vulnerability in my journal. My walls were intricate and masterful. I was so safe and protected behind them . . . limited risk . . . limited joy . . .

In the wee hours of the morning, I wakened to the words, "My light can't reach you." I knew I was alone, and yet I remained still and listened intently. Beyond the silence of the mountains and flowing nearby stream . . . clarity whispered again. "My light can't reach you. Remove a stone." He leads, I listen. Holy Goodness and Healing. This time, the sluice of tears presented renewal and possibility. I removed a stone, stepped into the sun, and felt hope for the first time in a long time.

I never saw the Woodstock gyrls again, but the catapult to healing was profound. My shift and return to joy wasn't magic; it would require persistence, strength, forgiveness, flexibility, and determination. "I couldn't possibly" responses expanded, and I met invitations and opportunity with "I couldn't possibly say no!"

This summer, my friend Julie, a fifth-grade teacher, was changing classrooms at the end of the year. Julie's example is one of availability. She leads with "yes" and pitches in all over town, at all hours, seemingly all the time. Isabella's wisdom echoed in my head, *Be who you're looking for* . . . I told Julie I'd lend a hand, and as soon as the words left my lips, I began to squirm. Cancelling was my recipe—not because I didn't want to help, but following through would leave me open . . . defenseless. Be who you're looking for . . . oh my. I showed up. The process proved so much more rewarding than moving books from one closet to another. My heart shifted.

Trust . . . just a droplet . . . a trickle, and then a stream became a flood of goodness washing me clean of my barriers of protection.

My road to discovery has been long and winding. I've walked countless hours over varied terrain enduring humanity's twisted sense of humor. I've learned shortcuts to growth and healing don't exist, and control is a mirage of wasted energy. Life's richness requires the pendulum to swing freely through seasons of grounding, seasons of isolation, and seasons of thoughtful partnering. The obstacles which changed my direction have taught endurance, perseverance, and escorted me to the path meant for me all along. His path in His timing.

I've learned the connections on the road to womanhood will surprise me, and I intend to move with appreciation, anticipation, and contentment. I'll no longer question why some links are made for an instant and others last forever. Each interaction's a gift that teaches, and the understanding is often beyond my comprehension. Connection is vital and becomes easier as we get older; our truest self is enriched with the wisdoms enduring, overcoming, loving, and healing have taught us.

White knuckles no more, I release my expectation. An open hand can be reached for, can be gripped . . . We are Stronger Together.

My pool of fulfilling relationships is expanding. The faces are new, humble, and authentic in a way I never dreamed. I encourage you to get out of your own way and dance. Continue to master new steps as the music changes. Be who you're looking for, and get ready because you WILL find them. Step into the vast capacity of your heart and share with others. Be brave enough to see yourself through their lens. Receive their kindness, and allow the weight to slip from your shoulders. No longer tethered, you will rise. *". . . chains are gone, I am set free . . . unending love, Amazing Grace"*

My friend Anne Marie provided an invitation to liberation when she said, "Regret no part of yourself. Something beautiful is happening." In my mind, I return to the truth table. I embrace my inner twelve-year-old and realize the most transformative piece for my personal healing. I abandoned her on the dark staircase. Healing in God's timing, by his design, requires Holy Patience and Trust. I ease back and speak gently . . . Dear one . . . Lift your eyes and see me, the woman you're **becoming**.

Hear me as I tell you, I've witnessed the power of connection. I've seen with my own eyes womanhood excited to bolster, uplift, and delight the deepest depths of your heart. Your walls of protection must crack so the light of healing can pour in. Trust me. I know . . . a hot button word, Trust. Will you try? For me? You were fierce, and you still are. You were passionate, and you still are. You were open and full of life, and you still are. You are me, and I am you. Your side road adventure, a merging of lessons and miles, is drawing to a beautiful close. Your body has changed, but so has your heart. You're ready to rejoin the path designed for only you. Shed the compromises. Shake off the weight of hurt, and layer yourself with forgiveness, pulling on the only armor you need. "The armor of Christ" (Ephesians 6:11). Surrender and make room.

Remember Who you are in this moment. Remember Whose you are always. You are no longer twelve. Your wisdom is rich, and your healing continues. You are a woman in progress, and it's time to leave the dark staircase. Get up now, take my hand, and allow your feet to be light as you join me in this moment we've made together. You within me will continue to propel my feet in confident directions. We'll continue to do big, confident, fearless things. ~ I love you.

"Regret no part of yourself. Something beautiful is happening." Our process to **becoming** is raw and real. Stronger Together, a connection I denied myself simply because I didn't know better.

The transformative, liberating, healing road of connection has returned me to the shoreline. I'm delighted to discover the vast sea of womanhood is bursting with bobbing Goddesses calling to me and inviting me in. I invite you to choose to move beyond the shadow of any protective barriers hindering your path. Lift a stone, place it beneath your feet, and marvel as your stumbling blocks become stepping stones. You are a Woman in Progress. Be who you are looking for.

Reach for outstretched hands. Link together, stand shoulder to shoulder, lean on, lift one another, and when you're ready, grab your floatie, noodle, inner tube, or unicorn and join us! Regret no part of yourself. We are Stronger Together, and We are **becoming**.

Nancy Mathieu

Co-Author

Nancy discusses secrets and what happens when that level of trust is broken. Secrets can become gossip that is shared outside the confines of a trusting relationship. Gossip can threaten to crack and shatter the very foundation upon which the relationship exists.

The Secrecy Code
Between You and I

Psst! I have something to tell you, but you have to keep it "between you and I." How many times has a friend declared this before they proceeded to tell you either a juicy secret, gossip about someone else, or a troubling revelation? Now the real question is how many times did it remain between you and them?

Gossiping is human nature. Men, women and children of all ages gossip to some degree. Sometimes it can be harmless, but other times (depending on what is being spread and to whom), it can be detrimental to your friendship.

One of my earlier memories of a "between you and I" bond being broken is when I found out I was pregnant. Most women (including myself) want to keep their pregnancy a secret, at least until they are out of the danger zone, which is approximately three months. It was especially important to me due to my family's cultural beliefs. We were raised to believe that it was bad luck to talk about the pregnancy to anyone except your partner, yet I was so excited to find out that I was pregnant that I wanted to share it with the world. So, against my better judgement, I decided to share my news with the person who was my best friend at that time. I called her and said I have something to tell you, but this must stay between you and I. Half-way through my announcement, she interrupted me to ask if it would be okay if she called me back in five minutes. It seemed odd to me because I was not even finished explaining the details of how I found out I was pregnant. I replied that it was okay for her to call me back, and we hung up the phone. She ended up calling me back a few minutes later to tell me that she had hung up because she had wanted to tell her mother my good news and that her mother said to tell me congratulations. I was speechless. She could not even wait till our phone call was over to go spread my secret. That was the beginning to the end of a longtime friendship. I realized then that she was not a trustworthy person to tell important information to. Some would say, "that's what you get for not keeping your mouth shut," but when you have exciting news and you are bursting at the seams to tell someone, you tend to go to your gyrlfriends. Same goes for bad news.

Ladies, when you are having relationship troubles, please pick and choose very carefully who you share that information with. Not all of your gyrlfriends want you to have a successful relationship, especially if they have a troubled relationship of their own or are single at the time. Some of them are silently praying that your relationship fails and may even give you bad advice to try to sabotage your relationship even more. A great example of some advice you may receive that I am sure you have all heard at some point before, is the old, "I would never allow him/her to talk to me or treat me that way. I would leave them if I were you." A person can never really say what they would do in a situation until they are actually in the situation themselves.

Most of the time, women are not really looking for you to give them advice. They are really just looking for a shoulder to cry on, a listening ear, or someone to agree with them. As a gyrlfriend, it becomes difficult to remain neutral because you can't help siding with your gyrlfriend, and you can even find yourself starting to dislike your gyrlfriend's partner, even if you've never even met them before. It's understandable. That's human nature. Unless your gyrlfriend is in a physically abusive relationship, then just listening to them complain is sometimes the best support you can give because, usually, the same person they are angry with and are complaining to you about today is the same person they are back in good graces within a few days. Now if they are in a physically abusive relationship, then all bets are off. In this case, giving advice and also breaking the secrecy bond may be necessary to protect your friend.

Just like there are different levels of friendships, there are different levels of secrets. When I first mentioned to my son Nicholas that I was writing a chapter for this book regarding the importance of keeping secrets, I think my son said it best when he said, "the only secret that's a true secret is one that you don't tell anyone!" I truly do believe that similar to the saying, "only lend money to others that you can afford to lose," that people should follow the following motto as well: "only tell a secret to someone if you would be okay if/when it gets spread around."

When it comes to friendships, I believe that the sharing of *some* of your secrets with others makes for a healthier and stronger gyrlfriend relationship. It's important for you to remember that the person revealing their secrets to you considers you a close enough friend that they are entrusting you with their darkest secrets. That friendship is made even stronger because the person receiving the information feels honored that their gyrlfriend is trusting them enough with their secrets. Sometimes, the sharing of some of your secrets lets others see that you are only human, not portraying a person without any problems or making it seem like you have the perfect life 100 percent of the time. As one of my closest friends said, "A true friendship is one where you know the other person's ups and downs and highs and lows." If you only share your stories of success, making your life appear wonderful all the time, while your gyrlfriends are sharing their trials and tribulations, then it is not a true, equal friendship.

Another important aspect of the keeping secrets that I think is very important to touch base on is keeping secrets after an argument between gyrlfriends. Ladies, if secrets are shared with you during a friendship, it is not okay to spread those secrets if your friendship ends with that person. What happens if you spread all sorts of stories about your former friend, and then your friendship starts back up? Being mature means understanding that even if you are no longer friends, the secrets stay with you.

Also ladies, if you hang out with a group of gyrlfriends and two of them have an argument and stop speaking, please don't feel the need to pick sides. Part of being an adult is being able to make your own decisions and learning to now balance the gyrlfriend relationships separately. Also, do not get caught up in sharing things that were told in confidence to you with the other person during a he said/she said session. It is easy to get caught up in the messy situation when all parties involved are not friends.

Years ago, I used to be very close to a friend I will call Mary. Mary introduced me to her cousin "Lisa." The three of us started hanging out together often. After a while, though, Mary decided that she did not like the fact that Lisa and I were getting very close and decided to give me an ultimatum. She advised me that I had to pick either her or Lisa but that I could not be friends with both. I chose Lisa because even though Mary and I did not have any issues between us, I did not believe in being pressured into kicking a friend to the curb. Now the trouble began. I had to worry about if that friend was going to become vindictive and spread secrets that I shared with her or be mature and just move on. If we all lived our lives with the "put the shoe on the other foot" motto, then maybe there would be less drama among gyrlfriends or ex-gyrlfriends. I try to put myself in the other person's shoes and think about how I would feel if something I told them in confidence was to get out now that we are no longer friends..

I only have a few close friends and those friendships mean a lot to me. I try to be there as much as I can for those friends, and I expect the same in return; after all, what are friends for! When I think of my close friends, I can count them on one hand. They are the ones I turn to when I have good news and bad news to share. I want to believe that I am someone that they turn to as well when they have their own good news or bad news to share. I take my friendships very seriously, and when those bonds are broken, it is hard for me to trust again.

One friendship that comes to mind that ended over what I feel is keeping secrets is one that I had with a friend of many years. We were very good friends, or so I thought. I shared with her, and she shared with me. We shared a love of baking, and I shared several of my recipes with her. I try to be very generous with sharing my recipes with my gyrlfriends, even after I have tweaked and then tweaked them some more. One day, I decided to ask my gyrlfriend for one of her recipes. Her response was, "I'd rather not." That response cut me to the core. It was not really about the recipe, it was about "keeping secrets." I could have found a similar recipe elsewhere, but what upset me the most was the response that came after that. When I pointed out that I had given her several of my recipes, her response was "and I appreciated that." Our friendship ended there. As time when by, I realized more and more that I felt betrayed. A friendship is not supposed to be one-sided. I felt that even if she was upset about giving me the recipe, she should have still handed it over to me without even thinking twice because she had several of my recipes in her possession.

If you are keeping something as simple as a recipe from me, then what else would you keep from me?

Another situation that comes to mind is gyrlfriends that keep secrets from you because they do not want to see you get ahead, or at least ahead of them. Is that really a friend, you ask? I ask myself that question all the time. I try to let things slide a few times, but after a while, I get frustrated enough that the friendship has to end. I can think of a gyrlfriend who tends to tell of opportunities only after the opportunity has passed or ended. Constantly telling me, "weren't you looking for such and such? I saw it on sale, but the sale just ended yesterday." Why bother telling me? The answer is because it gives you pleasure to know that you got a deal that I did not. The older I get, the more I realize that I cannot deal with the nonsense of keeping secrets. If I hear about an opportunity that I know would benefit any of my gyrlfriends, I try to let them know as soon as possible. Ladies, that's how we all get ahead. I truly believe what is meant for you is meant for you. Stop keeping secrets from gyrlfriends and help friends by sharing, and then hopefully, they will do the same. This will also make your friendships stronger.

I have been hurt and disappointed too many times to count, which has caused me to become guarded with who I am friends with and who I share my secrets with. Gyrlfriend bonds should be like having sisters. When you share private stories with gyrlfriends, you should not have to worry about whether that story is going to be spread around. When I tell you this is between you and I, then I want it to stay between you and I.

As I find my number of gyrlfriend relationships getting smaller and smaller, I am starting to look deeper into what makes me end friendships so quickly and not trust women as I should. I am finding myself either hanging out by myself more or only talking to the same few friends because I feel I can trust them. Don't get me wrong, I do not believe that everything I have ever told my best friends has never been repeated and vice versa. That would not be realistic on my part.

What I am saying is that I hope that I have picked my close friends wisely enough that they know the difference between important secrets and silly gossip. Harmless gossip is just that, harmless, but it is extremely important that a person can tell the difference and learn when what is being told to you is for your ears only. It is also important for you to be able to determine if what I have told you is something you should keep to yourself, even if I have not told you that it needs to stay between you and me. If I have come to you with information that I have asked you to keep between you and me, then that is exactly what I expect you to do. Please do not spread it around. And in return, I want you to know that I will try and do the same. Just know that if you entrust me enough to tell me important information that you asked me not to tell anyone, then I want you to know that I am not going to tell anyone. I want you to know that your secret is safe with me! Also, if you have told me something that I deem is important, I will keep it to myself, even if you have not asked me to!

As I get older, I am starting to re-evaluate my friendships and trying to take my own advice of also being a better friend to my gyrlfriends. I am now finally understanding that instead of dealing with drama, my way of dealing with the he said / she said is by ending friendships quickly and with no explanation. It is hard for me to trust anyone with my secrets because of being disappointed and hurt in the past by gyrlfriends, but I also realize that people need someone to talk to, especially if they are going through something. You can't be alone all the time; it is not healthy. I am sure you all heard the saying before: Sharing is caring.

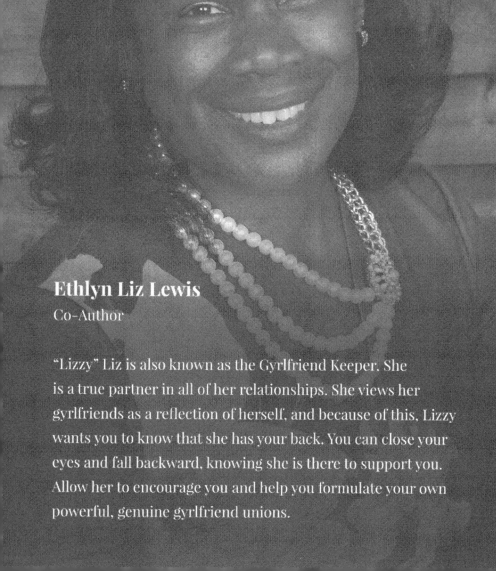

Ethlyn Liz Lewis
Co-Author

"Lizzy" Liz is also known as the Gyrlfriend Keeper. She is a true partner in all of her relationships. She views her gyrlfriends as a reflection of herself, and because of this, Lizzy wants you to know that she has your back. You can close your eyes and fall backward, knowing she is there to support you. Allow her to encourage you and help you formulate your own powerful, genuine gyrlfriend unions.

The Partnership Code
I Am My Gyrlfriend's Keeper

I'm a single mom with a 24-year-old daughter. I'm very close with my daughter; she is the very breath that I breathe. She's my little "Miss Independent" college graduate *(Shout out St. John University)* living in Brooklyn, New York, while I'm living the southern lifestyle. We don't get to see each other as much as we used to, but we maintain a close mother-daughter relationship. She shares with me the ups, the downs, and the most hilarious experiences she encounters daily. She also shares experiences from relationships with her gyrlfriends. Since we are so close, it is natural for me to share my own experiences with her in hopes of guiding her through handling gyrlfriend disappointments, which will occur. She and I call that "gyrl code." I am happy to be able to document our personal "gyrl code" as it relates to friendships. I've always been of the belief that my gyrlfriend should be also be my "sista-gyrl," a "ride or die" sister of choice. We share similar genuine values and sometimes mindset. She is someone I can count on through thick and thin, my Nettie *"Nothing but Death Can Keep Me"* *(The Color Purple)*. My "sista-gyrl" in her truest sense is the one who will never turn her back on me. She knows you are not perfect, and together, you do what you need to do to improve with her by your side. A connection with her is based on mutual love, respect, and consideration. A "sista-gyrl" has your back, and you have hers. This is the "lean on me when you're not strong" type of sisterhood.

Gyrl – Check My Pulse

I remember being the type of gyrlfriend that would fight my gyrlfriends' battles. Being very overprotective, if she had "beef" with other gyrls, we ALL had "beef" with the other gyrls. During the 1993 Caribbean Reggae club era, I can vividly recall standing in line, waiting to get in while dressed in "pum-pum" shorts. We were trying our best to appear cute for the security guards so they would not ask for our ID (we were underage). We not only got into the club, we took our lookalike selves (all dressed similarly) and proceeded to roll with the older, seemingly classier, "baller" woman. "Di Dance was sweet," (*like we say with a Caribbean accent*). After hours of partying, our crew left and headed back toward Brooklyn. Arriving at the after-hour diner for breakfast, I noticed one of my gyrlfriends flirting with the guy I happened to be dating. At the time, I didn't think anything of it as she was in a relationship of her own. I brushed off the initial thoughts that had begun to creep into my head.

Time went by, and I became roommates with the same gyrlfriend. During the period we lived together, I started to notice every time my boyfriend would visit, my gyrlfriend would make an appearance, having the need to leave her bedroom dressed scantily in nothing much besides a barely covering t-shirt. I felt uncomfortable. My boyfriend at the time felt uncomfortable, saying "you need to watch your friend, she's doing too much." Acknowledging his point, I agreed but did not act during this moment.

One evening, heading home from my job at Strawberries, I made plans to meet up with my boyfriend back at my apartment, not realizing he had arrived long before I had. As I opened the front door, he made his appearance, running out of "her" room. She quickly followed, wearing that same nasty "white" t-shirt. I can recall wishing someone would call "911." I was hyperventilating, ready to fight and take it to the streets of Canarsie, Brooklyn. I was devastated. How could someone I considered a "sista-gyrl" hurt me this way? We had shared so much together. We "were" virgins together; we were the best of friends. She was my "play cousin," my roommate, my "sista-gyrl." I picked up a frying pan that was on the stove and rushed toward her. Unfortunately for me, he blocked my attempt to give her the 1993 a** whipping I might still give her were I to see her today. Telling him to "get out," I just looked at her while retreating to my bedroom, slamming the door before sliding down to the floor to cry. I can never forget the look on her face; it appeared to me as though she were "smiling." I felt hurt by him but violated by her. In this moment, I lost all sense of being able to breathe and quite likely lost my pulse for a brief moment. This is the foundation of many of the trust issues I still have to this day with both men and women alike. This was not just any friend, though; she was someone I considered a "sista-gyrl." It was a double-whammy of betrayal.

Whatever Happened to the Original "Gyrl-Code?"

After my first experience of betrayal, I've always wondered whatever happened to "gyrl code." There are certain boundaries that women need to respect with other women. The most basic boundary frequently crossed is the violation of sleeping with someone's husband or boyfriend. Growing up in Brooklyn, we used to call it "branding." Once we "tagged" a guy or made comments like: "he's cute" or "you like him," the unspoken "gyrl-code" kicked in, signaling to your friends that this person was "off limits." Even if the guy wanted to speak with one of your gyrlfriends, the unspoken rule was in "effect" because you already expressed "liking" this guy. We would respect the unspoken code, knowing a violation would not be worth jeopardizing the friendship. Years went by, but we continued to honor and value the "gyrl-code." I've always had a genuine heart and much respect for my gyrlfriends. Knowing this, I could never cross that line and hope they in turn would return the favor.

Once, there was this time one of my married gyrlfriends' grandmothers had passed away. Distraught, she had asked me to check on her husband while she was out of town managing the necessary funeral arrangements. My automatic response without ill intent was: "No, honey, I'm not checking on nobody's husband. You need to do your best to prepare his food while you're away. He'll be fine." Again, I just didn't feel it was appropriate for me to tend to another woman's husband. It wasn't that I didn't trust him; I loved him like a brother. It was a matter of respect and not being willing to put myself in what could seem like a compromising position. With nosey neighbors looking on and fabricating false stories, it just wasn't worth it in my opinion. With the grace of God, and knowing my true heart, she understood, not initially seeing my perspective. Overall, sometimes it comes down to never doing to others what you would not want done to you. Always remember to treat people the way you would want to be treated.

I have tried to instill "gyrl-code" in my daughter and her gyrlfriends. I feel it imperative for the younger generation to feel this connection and understand the importance of character and the significance of trust. Trust has been difficult for me to regain. I am the one who loves hard and would fight for my gyrlfriend if needed. I would fight the mistress, fight the neighbor, hell, I'd even fight the kids disrespecting her. I know I cannot expect everyone to be like me, but it's important to know the depth of my respect for others, especially those I consider my gyrlfriends. Profession, finances, and educational status mean nothing without having that one confidante you can relate to and trust. I have had to remove certain people from my life who disguised themselves as gyrlfriends. Some of these are women I have known for over 30 years. But betrayal against me, my child, or someone I love are offenses not easily forgiven.

Gyrl-code is as sacred as the blood shared between sisters. We women need to understand that bond and be able to rely on one another for support. This bond enables us to say, "I need you gyrl," as well as, "Can we talk." It's not important that they agree with you. What's important is the bond shared between you. Within this bond, there are still boundaries, including what should be left as "pillow talk" between you and your significant other. Be careful about sharing intimacies in either direction. Personal, intimate stories your gyrlfriend shares should never be divulged with your significant other. Intimate issues between you and your significant other should also probably not be shared with your gyrlfriends. Although you should be able to share, some things are just better left unsaid.

This happens to be yet another violation I'd experienced with a gyrlfriend I'd known for over 30 years. Welcoming her into my home, my daughter even affectionately acknowledging her as an "aunt," in reference to her as an "Aunt," I introduced my gyrlfriend to a male friend of mine. During the course of their relationship, pillow talk included some very intimate things being shared with him about me. Knowing my genuine heart, my male friend relayed the betrayal to me. He ended his relationship with her around the same time I discontinued said friendship. Another level of betraying gyrl-code and not truly understanding the significance of this relationship, relationships between couples may come and go, but the relationship with a gyrlfriend has the potential to outlast them all.

Some of my relationships have not lasted the test of time. I've been told I am easy to "cut people off." Sometimes, for brief moments,

I wish it could be different, but for me, trust is the foundation for true friendship. When there is no trust, when morals differ, sometimes it's best to love them from a distance.

Distance is also essential in separating from negativity. Gossip is common, but when it's done with mal intent, it is a violation that proves destructive to "gyrl-code." When people have done nothing but good, and someone gossips about them, listening to the gossip is just as bad as telling it. We must hold ourselves accountable to our "sista-gyrls" as we hold them accountable as well. The support we have, the potential to gain from true sisterhood, is not just a rarity, it's priceless.

In the summer of 1997, my daughter was caught in a house fire while visiting with her sisters at their father's home. The woman of the house accidentally set the fire by tipping a candle over on an electric cable box and inadvertently attempted to douse the fire with water. During this time, my daughter and her little sister were both sleeping in the back room of the house. Initially, first responders declared them "dead at the scene," but God had other plans. When the second responder captain arrived, he commanded the team to continue trying to revive the gyrls. With God's grace, they survived the smoke inhalation. I was living in Atlanta at this time, working double shifts, when my gyrlfriend (my daughter's godmother) called me to tell me it was a story on the news. On the first plane to New York City, I arrived at King County Hospital's ICU within hours. Devastated beyond belief, I would not eat nor leave until I knew my baby gyrl was okay.

Childhood gyrlfriends brought me clothes, shoes, and underwear, ensuring I never had to leave my baby's bedside. I'm humbly grateful for that gyrlfriend support, for knowing when it's vital to "show up."

I can honestly say I have grown in many ways as well, "showing up" for the people many would consider the most unlikely candidates. Years ago, moving back to New York, I can recall receiving a phone call at one o'clock in the morning, filled with tears and despair. The caller on the other end was my daughter's father's (I don't use the term baby daddy) wife at the time. She called with the need of a place to stay after having a bad fight with our shared "children's father." Many thought I was crazy, my family thought I was crazy, as I allowed her to come over with two children in tow. All I could think was this was my "daughter's sisters" and women/mothers need to stick together. She had no one, and despite my failed relationship with my daughters' father, I wanted to be there for another woman, plain and simple. I wanted to "show up" and support another in need.

Support is priceless; sometimes we need to put aside differences and find a place of peace and closure. Nothing can determine your direction but you. I'm a woman of faith, and I truly believe "what goes around comes around." I want to know I have gyrlfriends that will support, encourage, and hold me accountable in my life's choices. No one is perfect, yet we can grow together. We are not in competition: We all can win.

You bring the cocoa butter, and I will bring the red wine so we can heal our scars as we laugh in the comfort of knowing GOD got us! We got each other! Gyrl-code!

Accountability Gyrlfriend

Several years ago, I was back in Atlanta, living a single life and embarking on the big 4-0. As I approached 40, I met someone, got engaged within eight months, then we got courthouse married in a year. He was what I would call a "Build-A-Brotha"; I tried to change him into a mature, loyal, caring, gentleman, none of which worked. It ended just how fast it started, to say the least. The lesson to be learned was never marry a stranger. My gyrlfriends didn't agree, but supported my decision to get married. At the time, I felt like I was going through a mid-life crisis. My daughter was growing up, getting ready to leave for college, and I didn't want to be alone. I have always tried to love people beyond their exterior, beyond their financial status, yet always remained the person most unappreciated and disrespected. Believe it or not, I've been engaged five times in my life, not always making it to the finish line. Everyone wants to marry Lizzy, yet not everyone wanted to do the work required of a husband. I was ashamed, even though I had the respect of my mother, my big sister, and my brother. At the time, even having the support of my family could not fill the emptiness felt from not having the support of a gyrlfriend. I felt I had no one I could call that would not judge me or let their protective emotions interfere. I felt alone.

Yet one day, I got a call from a long-time friend and caught her up on all my relationship drama. Instead of sitting back to comfort me, she held me accountable. She was brutally honest and told me "I NEEDED TO DO THE WORK," which meant taking a break from the "fast and furious" relationships. She was not afraid to tell me the truth. She was direct and genuinely worried for me, my daughter, and my health due to stress associated with these relationships. She saw the good woman in me and knew I deserved better in my life. Till this day, she has no idea how she has opened my eyes and changed my life. We both have busy lives now, yet we laugh and cry every time we re-unite with each other.

From my experience, we all try to rush "God's Plan" with relationships, whether with our gyrlfriend or a significant other. Yet, we need to hold ourselves accountable for where we fail.

In the first chapter, I failed accountability primarily because had I really looked, I'd see all the signs were there. The first sign was the disrespect I should have checked, letting gyrlfriend know it was a "non-negotiable" within our relationship. The second sign was the manipulation my boyfriend used to conquer and divide, coming between us gyrlfriends. The third sign was the failed relationship. A failed relationship may be a blessing in disguise and a part of what I believe to be God's plan. Your clock is not ticking, God has his own timing. My experience of marrying too quickly a stranger has not only been the biggest mistake but an opportunity. It allowed me the time needed to sit in the "PIT" of my life and do the work on myself. These experiences left me angry, hurt, embarrassed, and lashing out on all those I loved dearly, including my daughter. Thinking back, I might have believed my daughter didn't know something was wrong, but as close as we are, I'm sure she knew the pain I was in. This pain impacted my peace, my work, and pushed away my family. I was in a dark place in my life and blamed everyone and most importantly MYSELF. I was depressed, felt damaged, and broken—no good for anyone to love.

Now, in the present. My pain gives me strength. It has empowered me. I believe we must stand for something and fall for nothing. I am standing stronger than ever but will always relish having that genuine someone in my corner to lean on.

I Am My Gyrlfriend's Keeper

Mid-40's looks good on me. When I look in the mirror, I declare my peace and put me first before anything or anyone. It's MY time now. A time of new beginnings! Allowing myself to surrender and get baptized in April 2015 was my moment to cleanse myself. Giving me an opportunity to find the purpose God has for me. Sharing in this book is part of my GROWTH, surrounding myself around a season of positivity with no judgement.

I AM my Gyrlfriend's Keeper; I can trust again, including trusting that God will never give me more than I can bear. I can bare the weight of being my Gyrlfriend's Keeper. I can allow her to fall backward, being there to catch, support, and encourage her. I will hold her accountable as she holds me accountable. I got the cocoa butter for her scars. I will love on her as my "sista-gyrl," and if she rejects me, I will respect her choices. I will let her know that I trust in God's will, and He will return us together when it's the right season.

Let's dance; let's celebrate each other gyrlfriends. Let's accept each other's failures and encourage our successes. Let me say it once again, "We are not in competition; we can ALL win." Respect boundaries with compassion, and be transparent with our hearts, communicating with God in our spirit. Listen not just to be heard. Confide with trust. I wish nothing but peace, joy, and love in your everlasting life. In a place of love, hold me accountable when I fail you. Challenge me to walk with my head high; share your blessings for me to enhance.

You bring the glass, I got the wine.

Quote - Sweet is the voice of a sister in the season of sorrow - Benjamin Disraeli
Scripture — "For I was hungry, and you gave me food, I was thirsty, and you gave me drink, I was a stranger, and you welcomed me" (Matthew 25:35)

I Am My Gyrlfriend's Keeper

Painful tears may have burned my skin,
yet my healed soul allowed me to begin.
Chin'up my Gyrlfriend, take my hand in yours,
We have a destiny through those open doors . . .
I AM your keeper, through all the good and the bad;
No more, tears, no time to be sad . . .
We stand in our testimony, with direction from above.
You are my Gyrlfriend bonded by love. ~ **Ethlyn E. Lewis**

Cynthia A. Fontan
Visionary Author & Gyrlfriend Collective Co-Founder

Cynthia hid her depression for as long as she could remember. She is fearlessly coming forward to help others learn to peel back the layers and see beyond the superficial exterior. Cynthia will help us learn to be honest not only with others but with the ugly truths we sometimes hide from ourselves.

The Honesty Code
Not Without My Maskara:
The Modus Operandi of a Gyrlfriend with High-Functioning Depression

The Primer:

Gyrlfriends, we all have at least one of these women in our lives. She is the gyrlfriend that has it all together. She has a lovely, meticulous home; a supportive, loving, and very handsome husband; and a great career. You know her! She is fun to be with and makes you laugh. Her dynamic, cheerful personality and always polished image draws you and everyone she meets in. Her smile lights up the room. She is your gyrlfriend; the social butterfly and life of the party. She is smart, confident, and successful. She is your gyrlfriend; the one you go to for advice, your ride or die, the one you can depend on. Her drive and determination are something to be admired. You know where she came from and the hard balls life has thrown her way, yet she has endured them all. She is the gyrl that never lets you see her sweat. She works hard, always looks her best rocking the latest trends, and when she walks into a room, everyone knows she has arrived. You know her; she is humble and kind. She is one of your closest gyrlfriends.

Now, what if I told you everything is not always what it seems? What if I told you that her confidence and that aura of self-worth that she emanates is just a façade? Would you believe me if I told you that your gyrlfriend is putting up a front and hiding behind the fancy clothes and waterproof mascara so that you don't know what she is really feeling? Would you believe me then? It is true! This was me, your high-functioning, overachieving, always smiling, depressed gyrlfriend.

Gyrlfriends, I have been depressed for as long as I could remember, I would need to write an entire book in order to completely and fully demonstrate the many times and circumstances I faced that either exacerbated the depression or led me down a really dark place where the depression lasted for days or weeks. Those were extreme moments, however. I do not suffer from the kind of depression that we see on television commercials or in movies. I suffer from a form of depression that allows me to be high-functioning.

It sounds like an oxymoron, right? I thought so too! How could I be depressed when I go to work every day? I take care of my home and family, I have been in management positions with various companies, hustled several side jobs at a time while working full-time, been called an overachiever, and managed to finish school and graduate with two degrees. How in the hell does a person who is depressed manage to do that? Your high-functioning, depressed gyrlfriend that's who.

The Cover-up:

Gyrlfriends, where do I start my story when so many years of my life have been a blur? A combination of sadness, abandon, and hopelessness all mashed up together in a battle for center stage against the smile on my face, drive in my soul, red lipstick, black mascara, and great outfits (like the black leather pant and red sparkly sweater I wore to our holiday party and executive MPA student graduation celebration), but I digress.

Seriously, gyrlfriends, there is a thin line between sane and insane. Imagine you are walking on a tightrope connected between two skyscrapers in the middle of New York City. You are afraid to look down for fear of falling. You can't step to the left or to the right for fear of falling. The only thing you can do is stay focused on your goal and stay steady. You know you are walking this tightrope because every morning when you rise, you have to make the conscious effort to balance each step you take to stay in the middle, on the safe side of sane, when you'd rather lay in bed with the covers over your head hiding from the world.

Still, you know you have a job to do, responsibilities, and people who are counting on you, so you get up, makeup, and show up, right? That's what us strong women do, right? We go on pushing through wearing coverup to conceal the reality all in an effort to stay on that tightrope without losing balance for fear of falling into the dark side of insane. Staying in bed and drowning in tears processing the sadness is not an option. And, losing our sanity is not an option. Ain't nobody got time for that!

MasKara: Dressing Up and Showing Up

Like I wrote earlier, a lot of my life is a blur. I blocked out of my mind the times when depression was severe. Forgetting was the only way I knew to protect my sanity and shield myself from experiencing any more pain. Other people turn to drugs and alcohol, but I chose to block things out that hurt me. Doing this resulted in times of isolation when I didn't talk to anyone but those I had to communicate with, like my co-workers, husband, or family.

The first people I would isolate myself from were my gyrlfriends. I didn't talk to my best friend/sister from high school for years because of my depression. I didn't want her to know what I was feeling, and I was in denial that depression was real. So instead of telling her, counting on her to have my back, like she would, I pushed her away when I should have been honest with her and let her have the chance to understand what I was going through. I didn't give her the opportunity to be the gyrlfriend I know she wanted to be for me. Instead, I stopped communicating, put on my mascara, and went on with my life. That wasn't fair to her! Thank God, I was able to reconnect and reestablish our friendship without any damage.

For years, I discounted the truth that having depression doesn't mean in any way that I have failed myself. It means there is a chemical imbalance in the brain that makes me feel sad all of the time. So I went on living my life behind the makeup and fancy clothes so that no one would ever know. Wake up, makeup, dress-up, smile, pretend, cry, sleep, and repeat. This was my modus operandi for as long as I could remember. Cry at night, and shake it off in the morning was what I trained myself to do. It was what I saw my mother do and what I taught my daughter to do as well. Never let them see you sweat (or cry, or be sad) is what I told myself.

Still, I struggled with the reality of feeling a constant presence of sadness and hopelessness, and everything I did, even getting out of bed each morning, took monumental effort. Through it all, I felt like I was living a lie. The more I lied to myself about what I was feeling, the more anxious I got. At times, the anxiety weighed down so heavy on my chest that I thought I was having a heart attack. I would lose my voice and pretend that I had a sore throat. I didn't want anyone to know that I could possibly be having an anxiety attack.

The sadness and pain I was suffering started to manifest itself physically. I gained a lot of weight, and the sadder I got, the more I turned to comfort food. Food was my vice, and I'll end that right here. That part of my story needs a book of its own.

Lipstick: the brighter the lipstick, the harder for anyone to see through me, or at least that is what I thought.

About 20 years ago, one of my best gyrlfriends, a clinical social worker from Potomac, MD, confronted me about my depression. She said she could tell because I showed signs beginning with a lack of sleep. Since I didn't sleep well at night, I was often short with people. I had very little patience or tolerance for anyone who could not keep up with my pace.

I didn't want to hear what she had to say nor did I want to be diagnosed by my friend. Instead, I got angry with her and denied it. I told her she was wrong, and with a mix of tears and black mascara running down my face, I stood in front of her and proclaimed that I was too strong to be depressed and to beautiful to cry. Besides, I had way too many things to do like raise a child, work a full-time job, and hustle some side jobs because our lives depended on it. So, no, I didn't have time to be depressed and no way in hell was I going to let her know she was right. I knew I was depressed, but I wasn't ready to admit it or to seek professional help. I could manage on my own and I did. I kept the secret for the next 20 years.

As I continued to build my professional image, it was important to me to convey the message that I was a confident woman. What I didn't know then was the more I tried to ignore my feelings and hide behind this mask of perfection, the more distant I became. As a result, I lost

66

some good gyrlfriends because I refused to deal with the depression or tell them the truth. I was not that gyrl that had it all together. My life was a mess. All I did was cry myself to sleep every night.

Keeping friendships and nurturing relationships became more difficult as I got older, mostly due to my own fault. I felt I wasn't being authentic, so I'd rather not communicate at all. I was cheating those around me from getting to know the real me, depression and all. I didn't show them the vulnerable side or share with them that I was a gyrl uncomfortable in my own skin. I hid my feelings because I didn't want to be judged or misunderstood.

Gyrlfriends, can you feel me? Do you tend to hide your feelings? Maybe it's time to wipe off the makeup, maskara, and lipstick and get help.

The Exfoliating Cream: The Turning Point and Accepting the Truth

For as long as I could remember, I cried myself to sleep every night. I lived in a dark place and hid my true self. How could I tell anyone what I was really feeling if we had never talked about it? And if we didn't talk about it, how could they even begin to understand that I lived with an ever-present and constant sense of sadness and hopelessness, and everything I do takes monumental effort. Even meeting up for dinner or to a birthday celebration.

More times than I could count, I would have rather missed a family gathering than get out of my bed. Most often, all I wanted to do was hide under the white-feather down comforter and close myself off from the world. But still, the family was counting on me, and I was a strong woman who could handle anything, so I pushed aside my feelings, I got up, dressed up, and showed up. Late, but I showed up and pretended, once again, that I was happy and that life was great.

What my family didn't know was that even though I was in their presence, I felt alone, misunderstood, and at times, felt sorry for myself. They didn't know that telling me to "get over it" was not helpful. I couldn't get over it. I was depressed, and all I wanted to do was wallow in self-pity. But too bad for me 'cause I had an image to maintain, work to do, people to see, and a daughter to care for. Drowning in self-pity had to wait.

It wasn't until a very significant event in 2016, the passing of my mother, that I finally gave in, took off the mascara, and accepted the fact that I could no longer balance on the tightrope alone. I could not fight off the depression on my own any longer. You see, gyrlfriends, something happens to you when you are forced to watch your mother or any loved one wither away. This experience brought out the vulnerability and weakness I struggled so long to hide.

My mother suffered from Chronic Obstructive Pulmonary Disease (COPD) and was in an out of the hospital for years. She battled pneumonia more times than I could count. Her kidneys were failing, and her heart wasn't getting the oxygen it needed because her lungs were filled with fluid. The doctors tried many times to get her healthy, but she was tired of fighting. She was a breast cancer survivor, had a triple bypass, and was always sick with various ailments.

I watched as my mother died slowly and right before my eyes. The worse she got, the worse my depression got. But, again, I didn't tell anyone. Instead, I ate and ate and ate. Food was my comfort and my demon. It was my way of handling the depression besides hiding behind the makeup and clothes.

I carried on per my modus operandi until six months after my mother's death. My emotions took over me to the point where I cried at the drop of a dime for three months straight. Finally, my husband stepped up and said, "Enough!"

He told me he could no longer stand by and watch me cry uncontrollably. He acknowledged that I wasn't myself. He knew the gyrl that could cry all night and shake it off in the morning. He always said he was impressed with the way I could bounce back, shake of the sadness, and move on. But not this time.

I couldn't fight the depression on my own any longer. So I listened to him and sought medical attention. I went to my primary care doctor, and with my husband in the room, I openly talked about my feelings of

69

depression. When she asked me how long I had been feeling this way, I confessed, I'd practically been this way all of my life. Finally, it took my mother's death to get me to a place that I couldn't get myself out of to get help.

Wouldn't you know it, I was finally free of the secret. The burden of living a lie was gone, and I could be myself with some help. I was genuinely happy now because I told someone how I was really feeling and that I needed help. The weight of the cross I carried was off my shoulders, and the pain in my chest started to subside. My doctor prescribe a very low dose of Lexapro, a medication that works by increasing the amount of serotonin in your brain, which in turn, helps to decrease the symptoms of depression and anxiety. I have been taking it ever since, and thank God, I feel amazing!

The Gentle Moisturizer

If there is any advice I can offer to you reading this book right now, it's this: It is okay to get deep with your gyrl and ask her how she feels, but please be gentle. Think of the gyrlfriends that seem to have it all together (they are the ones that need you the most). It is okay to show your support, but if she is not ready to talk about her emotions, ease back. Don't take it personally and wait until she is ready. Remember to check in once in a while and bring up the matter again if you see she has withdrawn or has lost touch. That is the best thing you could do for your gyrlfriend. When she sees how much you care, she will let her guard down and trust that she can be vulnerable with you. She needs to know you will not judge her or think she is any less strong just because she feels down and out at the moment. She needs to feel safe and that you are there for her good. She will appreciate you just for showing that you care.

If you are like me and suffer from high-functioning depression then this message is for you.

Having depression doesn't mean in any way that you have failed yourself. It means there is a chemical imbalance in the brain that makes me feel sad all of the time. You can get help through medication or therapy, and you are not a weak person if you do. It is the exact opposite; you are stronger and wiser for getting the help that you need. You are taking care of your mental and physical self, and the clearer your mind is, the stronger you feel, the more you can do.

Remember that the more you ignore your feelings and hide behind this mask of perfection, the more distant you become, and chances are you may lose some really great gyrlfriends on this journey if you don't get the support and assistance you need. I lost some gyrlfriends because I refused to deal with the depression, and I didn't tell them the truth. I went into moments of isolation, and I didn't want to socialize or talk to anyone but my husband. I didn't want my friends to know the truth. I was not that gyrl that had it all together.

Depression does not define you or your future, and getting help will be one of the best things you can ever do for yourself. It was for me. Accept the past, live in the moment, and work on a better future you, darlings. Share your experiences with others and be the positive force you are meant to be!

~XOXO, Cindy

Dawn Ortiz
Co-Author

Dawn shares her story of living through and surviving infidelities within her own relationship. She hopes that these experiences, and the courage to share them, will help someone on their journey become stronger and resilient over time.

The Resilience Code
From Breaking Point to Turning Point

Gyrlfriend, we all have a breaking point of when enough is enough. Well, mine was when several intimate greeting cards were mailed to my home addressed to my husband. Can you imagine opening an intimate greeting card sent to your husband and reading the words "YOU MAKE ME HOT" written in bold letters. I know ladies, you said, "I'm going to kill that B*%CH," but that wasn't my response; after all, he was the lying cheat. I couldn't imagine being a woman who intentionally goes after a married man. No one could be that desperate for a man that in my opinion, they would want one who disrespects his wife and family. Or is it that the woman that believes his lies that he is so miserable at home, and they (the mistress) can make it all better? Do you really think he is going to change? Reality is that you believe his false promises because when I questioned him about the card, he said, "I don't know who she is, and anyone can get my information from the internet." Well, he may have believed his own lie, but I refused to. This was in fact my breaking point. It was time for me to end this marriage because after years of multiple affairs, I realized he would never change. But through the grace of God, I changed and got the courage to start a new life. I knew I deserved more and better in life. After all of this, I managed to raise three well-educated young ladies.

My Story

This may not be for the secure, strong, and independent woman who was able to say "Boy Bye." This is for the insecure women with three kids and is dependent on her cheating spouse. You got it. I stayed and thought things would get better, but if I was strong enough to believe the saying, "Once a cheat will always cheat," I wouldn't have been disappointed when it happened again and again.

Ladies, you can imagine my self-esteem was shot, and I began to wonder what I was doing wrong as a woman. I didn't feel pretty or attractive, and depression sunk in deep. But the most amazing thing was that no one knew, because on the outside, I put on a great show of this happy, wonderful woman who loved her life. My life looked glorious to others. I had three wonderful kids and a supportive husband, but inside, I was dying and hurting. For the life of me, I couldn't understand what I was doing wrong. I kept the house clean, cooked dinner, washed and folded laundry, and took care of the kids. Then, with all that, I still managed to love my husband unconditionally. This may sound crazy to others, but when you love someone more than yourself, it happens. As I continued to live in this nightmare with the hopes of change, I sunk deeper into depression. But I managed to hide my pain from family because, sometimes, family can make the situation worse without a solution to help, so I left them out and didn't share my pain with them.

It was my gyrlfriends whom I shared my pain with. Yes, we all have them "Gyrlfriends"; they are important, especially when you have problems with your man. They have so much to say. How about the gyrlfriend that would give you the advice to leave until they are faced with the same situation. And then there is that supportive gyrlfriend that would answer your call anytime of the day and listen to you rant about the same thing over and over. How about the gyrlfriend that means well but gives you bad advice that would have consequences? Bottom line, gyrlfriends are important; they help us get through any situation by just listening.

How God Kept Me in The Wilderness For 20 Years

This saying can apply to anyone for any reason in their lives. For me, it meant staying in my marriage in spite of all the extra-marital affairs. Yes, there were brief separations, but he always managed to make his way back in with false promises. But the bottom line was I was still trying to make this mess work for the sake of keeping my family whole. And if I can help anyone who is facing such a situation, don't let anyone judge any decision that you make. If they can't get you out of the situation, then shut your mouth and stop saying what you would have done.

It wasn't until the sixth year of my marriage I joined a church seeking God. No, I didn't leave, but my life changed drastically. God began to minister to my soul, and as I began to read scriptures and apply it to my life, changes began to happen. I know what you are thinking; he stopped cheating. The answer to that was hell no; he just tried to be less obvious with his cheating.

I changed my thinking, and as my pastor told me, "Don't look at what he is doing; concentrate on yourself, and ask God to change you." But I said, "I don't have a problem; I'm not cheating."

It wasn't for that purpose to stop him from cheating but to save my soul and deliver me from all that I was suffering from: depression, rejection, and insecurity. God wanted to help me get my life together for my three daughters that would someday want a family of their own. You notice I say God wanted me to change my life, although I wanted a change. I didn't know how to change until I invited God into my life. He was always there just waiting for me to acknowledge His power.

So for the next 12 years, it was me and God. Sure, I had a few dry spells in between, but I kept pushing because I knew my faith in God was keeping my head up. I'll spare all the details of how the cheating didn't stop, but I no longer paid it any attention because God gave me purpose. I didn't focus on my marriage. As long as he was still at home, nothing else mattered because to everyone else, we were a model family.

But that is not what God wanted. He is about truth, love, and honesty. Ladies, God wants you to have the life you deserve, but you have to be willing to sacrifice and trust God. I know when you are going through tough situations, especially when your husband cheats on you, it's hard to believe a God you can't see or touch. You would rather go out and get another man to hold and touch, but that's not the answer. That would only add to your troubles.

The Breaking Point

The gyrls are young ladies with college degrees and on their way to making lives for themselves. Finally! I didn't mention that my husband and I have been trying to work things out for the past four years. And yes, I was willing to put the past behind us because he finally changed. I said to myself it only took 20 years for this marriage to finally work.

I know you want a happy ending, but unfortunately he was at it again. This time, the woman mailed an intimate greeting card addressed to him. The irony of this is that I didn't have to dig or search for the truth; the truth came to me. The truth will always surface; just believe in the power of God. It's finally over!

My Final Thoughts

I am happy to say it was through the grace of God I escaped the wilderness unharmed. We all face unpleasant situations in our life, but it's how you go through it and whose counsel will you seek. I chose to seek God's counsel. In the Bible, Proverbs 3:5-6 says, "Trust in the Lord with all your heart, and lean not on your own understanding; In all your ways acknowledge Him, And He shall direct your paths." Abuse comes in many forms. I suffered emotional abuse, which can damage a person internally and externally.

Since I made the conscious decision to love God wholeheartedly, He made sure I escaped unharmed. Psalm 91:4 says, "He shall cover you with His feathers. And under His wings you shall take refuge, His truth shall be your shield and buckler." I am grateful that God has brought me to a place where I am physically, mentally, and emotionally independent.

Gyrlfriend code is essential to our wellbeing; continue to support each other, and don't hold back on sharing any thought that might help someone. We need each other; stick together because we are strong, successful, and beautiful. We are key players in society. Ladies, treat your body like a temple of God, respect yourself, and make wise decisions. I hope this reading has helped someone going through it in their marriage.

Dr. Melissa Noland Chester
Co-Author

Dr. Noland Chester discusses the various elements of success, with some being non-negotiable pieces of the puzzle. She expresses these non-negotiables as "Five Platforms." The rationale is when all five platforms are employed, the puzzle of success becomes an attainable goal.

The Success Code
Gyrlfriends' Solution to Success

A woman who walks in purpose does not have to chase people or opportunities. Her light causes people and opportunities to pursue her. – Unknown

Hello, Gyrlfriends! Welcome to the Potpourri chapter—this is the chapter that necessarily doesn't fit with the other identified chapters, but it's good stuff nonetheless! The information I want to share with my gyrls is information that can be applied to many aspects of your life—relationships, finances, and career and entrepreneurial goals. I know, I know. . . if it works, are **you** successful in **your** relationships, finances, and career and entrepreneurial goals?! The answer to that is . . . YES! When I apply ALL (not one, two, or a few), but all, of the principles I am going to introduce to you, I have great **success**. As I write this, I must admit that I have not consistently applied all of these principles; therefore, I have not seen the level of success I desire in my life. While others may think that I have attained success, I know that I have not scratched the surface of my capabilities.

As women making moves, on the move, or trying to get started, all of us are striving for **SUCCESS**. Daily, weekly, monthly, and yearly, we are reading, studying, working, and hustling to attain success. Well guess what, gyrlfriends?! I have the solution to success! But hold up, wait a minute . . . what in the world is *success?!* Let's take a minute to define it.

According to Webster's Dictionary, success is "a favorable or desired outcome." Dictionary.com defines success as "the accomplishment of an aim or purpose"; "the attainment of popularity or profit"; or "a person or thing that achieves desired aims or attains prosperity." The words that resonate with me as it relates to success are *desired outcome, "accomplishment of an [**one's**] aim or purpose."* So, in summary, *success* is a very **personal** and **subjective** word; therefore, success is a puzzle that has many solutions. What one may consider as success or being successful, another person may not.

With that being said, it is your responsibility to find YOUR own personalized solution to success! Let me say it once more for the people in the back: you must find YOUR own solution to success!

No matter what you are trying to accomplish or attain, there are some principles that are a must; these principles are my non-negotiables. I call these non-negotiable principles my *FIVE PLATFORMS OF SUCCESS.* A platform is a declaration of the principles on which one stands (Dictionary.com). In simpler terms, it's your design or plan to attain or accomplish **your** aim or goal. This means it does not matter if others feel you are or aren't successful, only what you think matters. The only person who can define success for you is you! With that being said, do **you** feel you've attained success?!

We must all employ the three Cs of life:

Choices, Chances, and Changes.

You must make a choice to take a chance or you will

never change. – Unknown

Before I talk about these five platforms I live by, I want to tell you why I chose to talk about success. When I reflect on the trials and tribulations I have overcome, and the many mistakes I have made in my life, I realize that the five tenets I am going to talk about soon were the reasons for my conquering every obstacle that has been placed in my life, either by circumstance or my own hand. As someone who grew up in poverty, has almost died twice, watched a man die, been molested (all of these happened before I was ten years old), and survived attempted rape and domestic violence (book coming soon), I know without a shadow of a doubt that it was GOD that kept me; He did so through instilling in me these principles that I try my best to live by.

As a child, teenager, and young adult, I did not know what these principles were, I just knew I always truly believed that despite my circumstances, I was meant to be more, do more, and be happy! After all we are human BEings, which means we are to constantly BE (continuous existence, occur, and take place). This means as long as we have breath in our bodies, we have an opportunity to be ANYTHING we believe we can be—BE happy, BE victorious, BE in a loving relationship, BE a great parent and BE successful! So I guess you can say at a very early age, I had an **IDEA** that things could and would be better, and I had the **MINDSET** that I possessed what it took to experience it. I did not know how this would happen, I just knew that it would.

I remember when I was a ninth grader in junior high school, and I was walking down the hall on my way back to class. One of our administrators was making an announcement that was for all free and reduced lunch students (which was the majority of the school). Although my sisters and I were eligible for free and/or reduced lunch, my mother's pride would not allow me to get free lunch. This means the announcement did not apply to me. The administrator was inviting the free and reduced lunch students to attend an interest meeting. The interesting meeting was for those that were interested in participating in a program that would assist you with going to college. The program was called Upward Bound.

Although I knew I was not technically eligible, I decided that I was going to attend the meeting anyway—I wasn't on free lunch, but I should have been! I attended the meeting, took the application home to my mother, and was accepted into the Upward Bound program. It is because of this program that I not only went to college but I went on an academic scholarship!

It is the first time I remember consciously implementing one of my principles—to **DECIDE**. I decided to attend that meeting. I made up in my mind that attending this meeting would get me closer to my dream of going to college. I often think about where I would be if I had not made the decision to attend that meeting.

One of the conditions of being accepted into Upward Bound was to commit to go to tutoring on Saturday mornings and spend six weeks of the summer on a college campus taking classes most of the day. I committed to doing so and had to exhibit **DISCIPLINE** and attend classes on Saturdays and during the summer. I did what I had to do from ninth to twelfth grade and was able to **PERSEVERE** through the program. The result of this discipline and perseverance lead to me applying and getting accepted into several colleges and obtaining an academic scholarship.

There you have it. My non-negotiable five platforms of success. **IDEA, MINDSET, DECIDE, DISCIPLINE, and PERSEVERANCE.** Continuous discipline leads to **PERSEVERANCE**. Let's delve a little deeper and really explore each of the five platforms.

The IDEA

No matter what people tell you, words and ideas can change the world. – Robin Williams

It all begins with an IDEA. An idea is a thought or suggestion as to a possible course of action (Dictionary.com). It is your belief, aim, or purpose. Oftentimes, ideas arise out of a desire to solve a problem. We formulate ideas every day; when we have an idea, we imagine or picture something in our mind that is in response to simple problems or societal issues. According to Napoleon Hill, first comes thought, then organization of that thought into ideas and plans, then transformation of those ideas and plans into reality.

One thing that is for certain, when you have an idea, you should first write it down. The word of God says, "write the vision to make it plain." Next you must act on it. This is the perfect time to give you a tangible example, so here goes . . .

When I was an undergraduate at Florida Agricultural & Mechanical University (FAMU) in Tallahassee, Florida, in the mid-1990s, my cousin and I came up with a fantastic idea. We decided we were going to create children's identification cards. We created a template for the cards with pertinent information on the front of the card like child's name, date of birth, height, weight, etc., and a picture of the child. On the back of the cards, we included the child's fingerprint and allergies. We developed our plan of action—during the spring semester we would purchase a laminating machine and camera, and during the summer, we would go to daycares, summer programs, and vacation Bible schools to solicit customers. We would call our company KidSafe ID.

When summer came, my cousin and I did just what we said we would do; we went around to different daycares, summer programs, and vacation bible schools . . . but we only did it for ONE summer. Although we had some success with our child ID service, for some unknown reason, we did not continue the business. We never discussed it; we just stopped.

Well, fast forward to the late 1990s, and one day, I was reading *Ebony* magazine. and low and behold, there were two young ladies being highlighted as up and coming entrepreneurs, and guess what their business was? Yep! That's right, children's identification cards! I called my cousin. and at first. we were BIG MAD; I mean, this couldn't be coincidence! These young ladies also went to FAMU and were making waves with the same idea my cousin and I had! After about an hour on the phone, we were laughing and cracking jokes on ourselves. At the end of the day, we could not be mad. It was no one's fault but ours that we had dropped the ball. Lesson learned. Having an idea is the easy part; it's the execution of ideas that are difficult.

MINDSET

If you think you can, you are right. If you think you can't, you are also right. - Henry Ford

The next tenet is MINDSET. Mindset is influenced by your faith and beliefs. The most important factors that affect your mindset is your attitude. Attitude is one's predisposition or a tendency to respond positively or negatively toward a certain idea, object, person, or situation. Attitude influences an individual's choice of action and responses to challenges, incentives, and rewards (Business Dictionary).

Your mindset, which is exhibited through motivation/ gratitude, is impacted by your attitude. Your attitude should not be influenced by others; it is **your** disposition or tendency. In order to maintain a positive mindset (attitude), you have to consciously make the effort. All of us have heard the saying "when you change the way you look at things, the things you look at change." A negative mind will **never** give you a positive life. You must start thinking positively in every situation you encounter. You must learn to be a thermostat and not a thermometer. Remember, your quality of life is at stake! I am going to share a story called High Expectations with you that was shared with me by Dr. Richard Ramsey:

Madeline Hunter, who has done a great deal of research on high expectations, advised her colleagues that she had found the solution to achieving high expectations. She told them that she wanted the opportunity to show them. She found a young lady fresh out of college with no teaching experience and wanted someone to hire her and let her mentor the teacher.

A high school principal agreed, but said, "nothing you do can help these low-achieving students." The principal gave the young new teacher the students with the lowest testing scores and the students with the worst behavioral problems. He did not tell her nor did the other teachers tell her; they were just glad the students were not put in their classes.

The young teacher begins to teach and teach each day with energy and enthusiasm. November came around, and there was not one referral reported to the principal's office. The teachers began to wonder and gossip in the teacher's lounge as to why things were going so well and why there were no problems with the students. One teacher said, "She must be giving them candy," another said, "She must be paying them."

February and March came and went, and still no problems with her students! The principal was curious about what was going on, but he didn't go down there. He said no news is good news.

State standardized testing time came and went, and the test results had come back. The principal had the test results on top of his desk, and the new teacher's class was on the top of the stack. He said to himself, "I know her class did poorly, and their scores are going to bring the entire school scores down," so he decided to look at them last. As he flipped through the test scores, he saw an average of two to three-point increases. As he began to look through the last set of test scores, he notices a 25-point increase in the new teacher's scores. He could not believe what he was seeing. He ran down to her classroom and quickly opened the door, and with a very harsh tone, he told her to step outside the classroom. She was very afraid thinking that she had done something wrong and would be fired. He said to her, "Your class test scores increased by 25 points; what did you do?!" She replied, "Nothing, sir," but the principal stated, "Please think back because I want to use your strategy with every teacher in the school!" She thought for a minute and then stepped inside her classroom and pulled a piece of paper from a stack on her desk and showed it to the principal. She said, "Look, sir, Tommie Walker, 200, Tameka Johnson, 190, Krisha Smith, 225 . . ." Then she said, "With these kinds of IQs, I expect my students to do well!" The principal, thoroughly surprised, responded in a loud and humorous manner, "IQs?! My dear, those are their locker numbers!" The moral of the story is high expectations [mindset] bring about high achievement! You must prepare your mind; when you change the way you look at things, the things you look at change! Successful people find a way to start *before* they're "ready"; we must understand success first starts in the mind.

DECIDE

The most difficult thing is decision to act, the rest is merely tenacity. The fears are paper tigers. You can do anything you decide to do. You can act to change and control your life. - Amelia Earhart

Now that you have acknowledged your idea and have addressed your mindset, you now must **DECIDE**. To decide means to "come to a resolution in the mind as a result of consideration" (Dictionary.com) or "to make a final choice or judgement about" (Merriam-Webster). To decide means **you must act.**

This concept is the most pivotal of the five principles. This is the one thing most of us have a hard time doing. Have you ever met people that always say, "I don't know?" It is because there is safety in those words. Once a person *decides* to do something, it is followed by actions. To ACT (Action Changes Things) is to change the trajectory of whatever *idea* you are contemplating.

Let's revisit the story about my cousin and my great idea about the children's ID cards. Well, we even did something with our idea; we decided to make it a reality. Unfortunately, we did not continue our actions. Remember, having great ideas is the easy part! What you do with the ideas is what matters. As Voltaire aptly put it, "Each player must accept the cards life deals him or her, but once they are in hand, he or she alone must decide how to play the cards in order to win the game."

DISCIPLINE

If being successful is your dream destination, you're going to need some extra doses of dedication. Because the greats will tell you, without hesitation. You don't win in the game. You win in the preparation.
— Dr. Albert Chester II

Okay, so now you have had a great idea, the right mindset, and you decided to act, but damnit, you still were not successful! Well, I can bet you the reason for this is because you did not possess or did not apply **DISCIPLINE**. Discipline is "to develop behavior by instruction and practice" or "training that corrects, molds, or perfects" (Merriam-Webster). Discipline is choosing between what you want now and what you want most (Augusta F. Kantra); it is the bridge between goals and accomplishment (Jim Rohn). It is restraint and willpower and correction and regulation for the sake of improvement.

Now, if there is one principle that I constantly and invariably struggle with, it is not my ideas, nor my mindset, nor even my resolve to decide to act. I constantly battle (along with the majority of society) with my lack of consistency and inability to stick to my daily habits. There have been sooo many times when I had an idea and the mindset that I possessed the ability to bring my idea into fruition, but because of a lack of focus or consistency, I was not successful. This lack of consistency and focus is because I did not have enough **DISCIPLINE.**

Discipline is to consistently decide to do what is necessary or required to attain a certain goal. I have realized that my biggest issue in some areas of my life is discipline; especially as it related to consistency and daily habits. Discipline is the sum total of commitment, consistency, and daily habits.

Daily habits determine success or failure. It is best summarized in this quote by my colleague Sam Hall, "Greatness is *not a state* of being. It is a *process* built upon *repeated behaviors* that become [daily] habits of greatness; therefore, to BE great, one must first *BEcome* great!"

Will Smith has a great session where he talks about discipline. He explains it in the simplest terms: self-discipline equals self-love. I heard this quote on YouTube once that said a major cause of failure is because your life is ruled by randomness. If you are chopping a tree, and you chop it a hundred times in a hundred different places, you will never chop it down!

Discipline incorporates the understanding that today's activities will produce tomorrow's results. Discipline is dedicating yourself to the most positive use of the present. So why not "do it today because tomorrow is often the busiest day of the week." (Spanish Proverb)

PERSEVERANCE

"The key to success is action, and the essential in action is perseverance."
– Sun Yat-Sen

Lastly, we have **PERSEVERANCE**. Perseverance is simply steadfastness or not giving up. Discipline and perseverance go hand in hand. Without discipline, you will not persevere; without perseverance, you will never develop discipline. Perseverance is the "continued effort to do or achieve something despite difficulties, failure, or opposition" (Merriam-Webster). "Life is a fight for territory. Once you stop fighting for what you want, what you don't want automatically takes its course" (Michael McGrone). It is steadfastness despite difficulty, delay, or failure. As Walter Elliot so aptly put it, "perseverance is not a long race; it is many short races one after the other."

I constantly debate whether discipline or perseverance is the most difficult habit to develop. While discipline is employing daily habits and consistency, perseverance is endurance and finding the strength to continue. When your discipline fails, it is perseverance that keeps you going and prevents you from giving up. When talking to people who consider themselves successful, 90 percent of them spoke on endurance and perseverance. We have all heard stories from famous and not so famous people speaking on *almost* giving up . . . how the one last time they decide to persevere ended in success.

Whenever I need a little burst of motivation, I look at the picture of a man digging for diamonds, and right before he reaches them, he gives up and turns around. When I feel like giving up, I look at the picture of Jeff Bezos, Founder & CEO of Amazon in his office in 1999 (Google the image, it's a must see). It is the ultimate example of commitment and **PERSEVERANCE**!

Despite numerous obstacles and trials in my life (I mentioned them earlier), I consider myself successful. There have been many instances in my life where if I had decided to give up, my trajectory would be very different! One example of this is when I lost my academic scholarship and financial aid at the end of my sophomore year. I ended up sitting out of school and working at Subway as a sandwich artist (I am probably dating myself with that one). I was out of school for a year and a half and had to pay for a semester out of pocket (which meant I took out a loan because I was ineligible for financial aid).

I ended up getting back in school and working very hard to raise my GPA and graduate. The semester I was kicked out of school, I had a 0.75 GPA (no, it's not a typo); I ended up graduating Cum Laude (taking as many as twenty hours one semester and sixteen hours during the summer). If I had given up at that point, where would I be today? I had failed, but I refused to be a failure. I persevered and got my first of three degrees. Through perseverance, many people win success out of what seemed destined to be certain failure (Benjamin Disraeli). Success isn't in the giant leap; it's in the daily discipline and persistence one employs. It is endurance and commitment. The race is not given to the swift, but him who endures till the end (King James Bible).

FIVE PLATFORMS OF SUCCESS

"The road to success and the road to failure are almost exactly the same." – Colin R. Davis

There you have it ladies! **MY** five platforms of success: Come up with an **IDEA**, Embrace the proper **MINDSET**, **DECIDE** to act, Learn self-**DISCIPLINE**, and exercise **PERSEVERANCE**. I get it; it is too much or too difficult because it's a lot, right?! Trust me, I get it. I get it because I have been there.

When I feel myself getting overwhelmed, I use the philosophy of "turning an elephant into an hors d'oeuvre." This is one of my favorite sayings because it makes so much sense! The reason people are not "successful" accomplishing their goals is because they are trying to eat the entire elephant instead of chopping that big boy up into bite-size pieces!

Let's take my decision to create the national educational nonprofit organization, Black Educators Rock, Inc. What an elephant this was (and still is)! This growing nonprofit started from an *idea*, and it wasn't even mine! My former college student contacted me and told me he had an idea and wanted to start a Facebook group for educators in order to support each other and share resources.

His *mindset* was that he and his fellow educators needed the site, and by having it, it would help them be better educators. It turns out, he was absolutely right! In one day, there were over 1,000 educators in the group. In four months, the group grew to over 100,000 educators all across the country and abroad! This is when I stepped in.

I informed him that the organic growth of the Facebook group shows there is a real need. Educators need encouragement, support, and resources. I *decided* that we must create a nonprofit and be more than just a Facebook group. And we did.

From that decision, we created Black Educators Rock, Inc. We also decided that one of our primary focuses would be an annual summer conference, with the goal of the summer conference being to ignite the fire in a teacher for the new academic year. I knew that it was going to take discipline/commitment and perseverance to grow the organization and reach its full potential.

It was my student's *idea,* and he had the *mindset* that the Facebook group was very needed and it was his job to create this space for his fellow educators. Together, we *decided* to create a nonprofit. After our inaugural conference in July 2016, my student decided he couldn't continue to work with the organization. Now I had to *decide* if I was going to continue to work with an organization that wasn't my idea.

I am the one that exhibited the *discipline* and *perseverance* to continue to make Black Educators Rock, Inc. the preeminent educational member nonprofit across the country and abroad (it's a work currently in progress). In my heart of hearts (isn't that a weird saying?!), I truly believe this is the solution to success! If a person puts these tenets to practice in their relationships, finances, and career/entrepreneurial goals, they will see definitive improvement in these areas. Now, it's your turn. Get to work and turn the elephant into hors d'ouevres.

Maureen Carnakie-Baker

Visionary Author & Gyrlfriend Collective Co-Founder

Maureen encourages women to identify the source of their conceptions about money. She also anticipates this to be the beginning of inciting open, ongoing dialogue on finances and the impact it has on all relationships not just those between gyrlfriends.

The Financial Code
Counting Her Coins

I can vividly recall being ten years old, standing by, helplessly watching my mother mentally tabulate. Mother was counting loose change that had been emptied out of one of those vintage coin purses with the clasp at the top. Pensively, I knew she was calculating what groceries she'd be able to buy to feed a family of six, five of us being children. Looking on, I remember thinking: "whatever she buys, don't complain" and with childish faith, "that will never be me." To this day, those thoughts continue to drive me, dictating my choices and fueling what seems to be a perpetual pursuit of financial freedom.

My parents had just separated again for what would become the last time. Although my mother came from a moderately middle-class family (some with homes that should be paid off by now from years of rental payments that even my mother made), here, she was trying to figure out how to piece it all together on her own. I did not know then, but found out much later, how much my older sisters (ages 18 and 19 at the time) and my present-day brother-in-law stepped in to help out.

When kids at this age should be thinking about what they're going to buy with the money they earned this past week from their part-time job, my siblings were contributing part of their checks, bringing home groceries, and helping to make sure life's necessities were provided. They were becoming self-sufficient and marrying for better or worse (in some circumstances). They went without new shoes and missed prom so the younger ones (myself included) had what we needed.

I didn't know then that from their perspective, moving out was an opportunity to alleviate some of the financial burdens my mother experienced, having two less mouths to feed. I am forever grateful for the sacrifices made by all of my siblings and those of my mother. Understanding as an adult that although one can try, they can never fully repay for sacrifices they are aware of nor the ones that only become apparent with time, age. and bills of one's own.

Using the experiences I've encountered, I hope to remove stigmas associated with talking about finances (specifically money and/or the lack thereof) and positively transform our discussions on money and its impact on our relationships.

Financial stress and money have always been thought of as one of the top three reasons most couples get divorced, trailing pretty closely behind infidelity and communication issues. Considering it's one of the top three reasons relationships fail, it is bound to also have a profound impact on the dynamics between gyrlfriends.

Counting Her Coins

Just as my mother counted out her coins to assess affordability when it came to an everyday staple, many women, without being deliberate, mentally do the same. We tend to size up both men and women and see if they can afford our time, our friendships. We assess one another based on profession, as well as other superficial traits, including but not limited to material possessions and outward appearances.

What's one of the first things people usually ask when they meet someone? What do you do for a living? I've often wondered why many of us feel being in the "know" about what someone does for a living will also reveal substantive information about the person. Instead of pondering whether or not this is someone we'd actually enjoy being around, we make assumptions about size. Because in our minds, size really does matter, at least as it pertains to someone's wallet. In actuality, the only deductions we can potentially safely make based on one's profession may include the types of tasks they carry out on a daily basis, and even that may be a stretch unless you're employed in the same profession. And yes, we also have this same tendency amongst gyrlfriends.

Over the years, I've run into various situations with strangers and friends alike where you can almost see the wheels in their heads turning, summing up how much they believe someone has and can afford. They also tell themselves stories about what they believe someone may not have as it pertains to finances. This phenomenon runs both ends of the spectrum.

One of my closest gyrlfriends for over 20 years encounters this often from the perspective of "having." Founder and managing partner of a healthcare technology investment firm, "Darlene" has done extremely well for herself. Raised in Jamaica by a teenage mother, she emigrated to the United States, working for various consulting practices, before saving enough to attend medical school. Since then, she has gone on to build a thriving biotechnology firm that now invests in healthcare technology startups.

Darlene's pedigree supports my theory of small sacrifices (coupled with diligence and opportunity) having the potential to yield substantial results. Earning a seat at the table by her own merits has brought her a sense of pride, accomplishment, and a great deal of mistrust for those closest to her. Casual events, including the spontaneous meet-ups with extended family members during her travels, has a way of morphing into four-course meals paired with a hefty tab that everyone naturally assumes it's only fair that she picks up. While those seated at the table were eager to browse and select from a menu without giving a second thought to cost, this same effervescence turns into awkward silence and polite excuses from the table when the waiter appears with the check. This is but one instance of others automatically making assumptions based on preconceived notions about one's profession and, subsequently, their financial status. You can almost hear the thoughts in their head, "She got it; let her pay the bill. This is a drop in the bucket for her." How nice of them to mentally "count her coins" never once feigning the polite reach and offer to pick up the check.

Drawing from my own experiences, I will never forget the season I managed large-scale summer medical conferences in three locations across the country, overseeing operations 16 to 18 hours a day over a three-month span. My only solace during this time being the occasional pleasure trip to a local mall 15 minutes away.

During one of these therapeutic retail breaks, I wandered into one of my favorite stores, Michael Kors, a small boutique I could explore relatively quickly. Ensconced on one of the alluring white shelves, I spotted one of the most supple, elegant, black leather handbags I'd ever seen. Asking to see the bag, I quickly glanced inside first, attempting to ensure it was within my means before proceeding to fall in love. To my surprise, it was within reach.

Quickly asking the sales attendant to ring it up, I started to count out the cash to pay for my purchase. One hundred, two, three hundred. As I continued to count, and the attendant remarked on the bag's beauty, a female patron expressed her agreement and watched as the attendant proceeded to delicately wrap my purchase. Almost without hesitation, the female shopper inquired: "Do you mind me asking what you do for a living?"

Now, I know I was dressed the part, as running conferences entailed the frequent interface with deans of medical schools, as well as clinicians who served as keynotes. No matter what the reason, I was caught quite by surprise as this woman thought nothing of "counting my coins." Almost 10 years later, the memory remains, and I contemplate why she felt obligated to query my ability to afford this sliver of luxury. What was her intent? Some may feel this is paranoia at its best. But just as possession is 9/10 of the law, the same can be possibly said for intent.

In efforts to avoid questions and comments being misconstrued, the takeaway simply goes back to the age-old idiom: "How would you feel if the shoe were on the other foot?" Stop and, for a brief moment, think before speaking, asking yourself: Would I want someone to ask the same question of me? How would it feel if I was always expected to pick up the tab for everyone? And even when the answer to both of those are yes, you're okay with it, don't assume that if you are, the recipient will be too. Money is a tool to be used. People are not. Avoid counting her coins, making assumptions, and creating greater distances between us.

If you're going to have genuine discussions about finances and money, make sure the playing field is leveled for both parties.

The Takers

The idea of leveling the playing field, with all things being equal, is really just that—an idea. Quite the norm, there are more variances between us as it pertains to gyrlfriends. One of us may be married and have that second income to rely on, whereas the other may be bootstrapping it on her own as Miss Independent. Both of us can have great professions with similar incomes and still experience differences as it pertains to lifestyle.

Is it possible to maintain friendships when you're used to splurging on a whim and your gyrlfriend is struggling just to keep the lights on? Absolutely, but here is where empathy and setting expectations (most of which should go without saying) will come into play during the course of that relationship. These differences are likely to impact everything from the social events you choose to attend together to milestones experienced including marriage, having children, and even owning businesses.

All relationships should be reciprocal in some way. Not that it has to be "tit" for "tat," but everyone should walk away feeling whole and as if they are a better individual because of that relationship. Why would the relationships we share with our gyrlfriends be any different? One should be able to lean on the other in times of need and in times of joy.

But leaning and occasional support does not mean throwing your full weight on the other person, never once asking if they themselves are okay. Support goes both ways. One-sided relationships fueled either by selfishness, disregard for the other's feelings, or even sometimes greed has the potential to breed resentment, ruining the strongest of friendships. "Takers" in a relationship are usually incapable of seeing anyone's perspective but their own, presenting almost as a sociopath would (okay, maybe that is a little extreme) with a lack of conscience.

Here are some ways to identify the "Takers" in our lives and relationships as it pertains to finances.

You might be a "Taker" if:

- You always want to hang out, but when the bill comes, you either go ghost or you quickly say: "You got me?" How in the hell do you leave the house being broke when you knew you were going out to eat? Furthermore, just because someone asks you to go out with them, it does not mean they get to foot the bill. It doesn't work like that. Not in this world. Not in any world. Never once offering to pay or reach into your pockets or perhaps just opt out of drinks considering at the end of the day, even though I was mindful about keeping the bill to a minimum, you were throwing them back. Who does that? That's a "Taker."

You might be a "Taker" if:

- Someone does offer to take you out and pick up the bill. Not only do you go and enjoy your meal and the pleasantries shared but at the end, you ask for "another meal to go" for later or for someone waiting at home.

You might be a "Taker" if:

- You are an expert at creating "Go Fund Me" pages in the blink of an eye to support your latest trip or your newest project but never seem to fund anyone else and their endeavors. We see you, and we're keeping our distance.

You might be a "Taker" if:

- You borrow money without the intent of ever repaying the loan and avoid bringing the subject of the loan up at all costs. Matter of fact, you try to deflect and channel the person's attention elsewhere.

But here's the raw truth as it relates to friends and money changing hands. Do not lend what you cannot afford to give. That is the "truth in lending" statement. Similar to when you borrow money from the bank to purchase a home, your mortgage comes with a "Truth in

Lending Disclosure." Once you sign on that dotted line, you need to be aware that although the bank is willing to loan you this cash, the interest associated with the loan is high. You may forfeit the house if you do not repay the loan. And in the case of gyrlfriends, you may forfeit the relationship.

I, myself, have experienced forfeiture of a long-standing friendship as a result of someone being unwilling to read the dotted line. Always making sure I present as "Ms. Independent," others closest to me noticed too and developed a tendency to lean on me in times of need. Being someone who is extremely selective about those in my tight and small inner circle, I loaned a large sum of money to this gyrlfriend of many years without hesitation. Along with this request for this loan came her promise that the money would be returned as soon as she was on her feet.

Several years later that spanned her celebratory birthday trips to Las Vegas and the purchases of new puppies, I have yet to receive the full amount loaned. Was this addressed? Yes, it had been requested both verbally and in writing, but to this date, I have yet to be made whole. What I have in its place is a better understanding of how expectations need to be set, even amongst the closest of friends.

I've also learned that not all relationships are meant to last. Some will blossom while others fade. Sometimes, we've outgrown the relationship, and it's important to recognize and be okay when or if that occurs. Sometimes, we sever the relationship because as we grow, we realize the relationship is not yielding our investment.

Time, energy, feelings are all investments we make. When there's minimal or no potential Return on Investment, all the investor ends up with is a feeling of being used. At the end of the day, you don't have to be a CPA to CYA (Cover Your Assets). Although our focus has been on finance and money as it pertains to relationships, your greatest asset is always going to be you. Remain true to who you are and be comfortable with those you surround yourself with. Make sure your assets (thoughts, hopes, dreams, finances) are nurtured, respected, and valued. This value and respect starts with you and how you perceive yourself.

In many ways, gyrlfriend relationships are like scrumptious potluck dinners prepared by the greatest of chefs (all hand selected by you). Before you sit down to dine, your succulent feast starts with a sense of confidence, knowing you've made your finest dish. You've prepared your best, earning your seat at the table. Your only expectation is that your guests (your hand selected gyrlfriends) also put their all into their contributions, leaving you satisfied, feeding your soul.

Steps to Improving our Gyrlfriend Relationships

Change the narrative.

Instead of asking what do you do for a living, instead ask what do you enjoy doing in your free time?

Create a schedule where you can nourish those relationships via dinners, meet-ups—with everyone taking a turn at hosting. Understand and appreciate what someone can bring to the table.

Be honest and transparent about loans. Discuss timelines associated with expectations for repayment. If you know they would never be able to repay, gift what you can afford to give. If you cannot afford to gift it, be comfortable with stating you're unable to assist.

If the relationship is starting to feel one-sided, express your feelings about this. No one likes to feel used, but sometimes "takers" may not know they are perceived as "takers."

We are never too old to make changes and that includes our perceptions about money and people. Money is a form of currency, a medium of exchange with both sides bringing something to the table that the other walks away with and still feels whole.

Dr. Tricialand Hilliard
Co-Author

Tricialand wants us to know that we are continually growing into our purpose. Your purpose may not always allow you to be with the same group of gyrlfriends all the time. A true gyrlfriend will understand that and call you to connect with you about you. They will know that while life is happening, and you are growing, she is still there for you, rooting for your "rise." Tricialand will help you discern who "roots" for your rise and who does not.

The Maturity Code
The Grown Gyrlfriend

The Evolution and My Growth: Piece by Piece

Gyrl, listen! Let me tell you. I hope you are ready for this tea.
Warning: *Sip slow as not to burn your mouth!*

I know you have heard women say, "I am who I am," or, "I'm not changing for anybody, take it or leave it." The truth of the matter is women are ever-changing. We wear so many hats and function in various arenas I cannot even begin to list them all. So, the validity of those statements is so far from the truth. As I have lived, I have grown to see how change it necessary. So change does not only pertain to me but the people and relationships around me. Did that statement burn the back of your throat? I am sure that was hard to swallow. I am going to give you some time to PAUSE, and think about the questions I ask.

FACT: As we change, our friendships should change. Meaning, the gyrlfriends in the relationship or the relationship with the gyrlfriends.

PAUSE: The question is, "Are you willing to change?"

Research shows that women think all the time. Especially more than men. This explains why women overthink things. I swear . . . I

117

wake up thinking about anything and everything. This is after I can quiet my mind enough to go to sleep. I have a million things on my mind all the time. I think about work, my partner, my parents, my money, my hair, and most of all, my relationships with my gyrlfriends. These things have caused me pleasure and pain. But gyrl, over the years, I have learned to say the serenity prayer before I go to bed to put my soul to rest to reduce my stress.

FACT: Sleep is a part of the primary factors of basic functioning.

PAUSE: The question is, "Are you so worried about others that you neglect your own self-care?"

I was a victim, but I am a self-care survivor now. I used to worry and work myself to the ground by always saying "yes." But 2013 was my year of "no." I am not going to lie, it was hard, but it was the best thing I could have ever done. I had just broken up with my boyfriend, my parents chronically ill, trying to buy a house and looking for a new job, and entering into my Doctoral program. To put it lightly, I was overwhelmed but did not know it. Or rather, did not want to admit it.

If it was not for God and my gyrlfriends, I would not be here. My two best gyrlfriends intervened themselves in my busy life and took me away. Away from all of the million little things that my mind was wrapped around to just focus on me. We went down to one of my gyrlfriends' family beach homes and stayed the weekend. We cooked, sang, watched all episodes of *Sex in the City*, *Girlfriends*, and *The Color Purple*. We just had an old-school sleepover. Plus we made vision boards that took two days to complete. This communion and fellowship was needed for me to get my thoughts together to reevaluate my priorities and give myself permission to say "no" to others and to say "yes" to myself.

FACT: As women, we are the natural caregiver in various aspects of our lives.

PAUSE: The question is, "Are you willing to sacrifice yourself for others?"

Over the years, I have realized that in order to fulfill your purpose here on earth, you must take care of yourself. I feel like I have learned that I can't fulfill my purpose alone either. I know this tea maybe hard to accept, but it's true. According to God, you cannot fulfill God's purpose by yourself. God wired us to need each other (Pastor Rick's Daily Hope). Understand, needing others does not always allow you to be with the same group of people or "gyrlfriends."

I know, I know, this may mean you are being "fake" or "being 50" with your old high school gyrlfriends or the church gyrl group. These groups are often changing because you are changing as you grow to know yourself. Similar to the trees during the seasons, which you use to identify where you are during that period of time in your life.

FACT: Evolution is a theory based on the species' ability to adapt to the environment and survive. Change is the only thing that is constant in life.

PAUSE: The question is, "Are you able to be true to yourself and leave some gyrlfriends behind to achieve your purpose?"

Gyrlfriend, Listen Here . . . A True Diehard Gyrlfriend is the one that will be there when you call and not ask you a million and one questions to try to turn the situation around and make it about her. I am sure we have all heard this from a gyrlfriend before, "Why haven't you called me," or, "Where you been?" Or my favorite, "I thought we were 'best friends.'"

The first thing she SHOULD ask you is "Are you okay," "How you been," or "What do you need?" This is a true friend who loves you: I mean all of you, the evolution of you. This true gyrlfriend understands that life is happening to you, and she is mature enough to be there for you by rooting for your rise.

FACT: People are forces of energy in human form. In life, gyrlfriends either add to you or subtract from you.

PAUSE: The question is, "Which one are you, and which type of gyrlfriend are you?"

YOU SAY SHE'S JUST A GYRLFRIEND

You've picked up this book because you're a gyrlfriend. Well, so am I. See, we will already have something in common. Maybe after reading this chapter, you can decide whether we can be gyrlfriends. Yeah right, I wish it was that easy. I wish we could get all the information on a perspective gyrlfriend. I would love to get a gyrlfriend's resume upfront. If accepted, I would probably make her complete a three-part interview: phone, round one interview, and round two panel interview. I am joking, but I am probably as serious as a heart attack.

I take being a gyrlfriend very seriously. I would go as far as making the second-round interview a panel of the different versions of my selves: past, present, and future to see if she is really down for the cause of me. I need to know if she can take all the pieces of me. Come on now, you know you are not the same person you were five years ago. Let alone two years ago today. I believe if a gyrlfriend could stand an interview with all the different versions of me, at one time, then she is a keeper.

I'm not sure if I could even make it through an entire interview with my future self. Could you? You already know your future self would have so many plans for you to do; you would not be able keep up with you. You know I am right. Because if I am lying, then why are you already making plans to attend the January 2019 "vision board party," and its only September 2018. As women, we plan for our greatness at all times. Even four months in advance. So at least the gyrlfriend interviewing for the position of "my gyrlfriendship position" would know how serious I would be. The ad would probably read:

Open position:

Who can deal with me? Is it you? She MUST able to deal with ALL of me. The parts of me I cannot even see sometimes. The parts that often hide in the shadows of my well-dressed, masked self that I present to the world. Can you see my soul wounds under the make-up that I wear? I hope you can, but I won't openly show you because I am guarded. Note sometimes, I have to be guarded to survive. I hope my gyrlfriend can help me, I mean really help me. She needs to be the type to provide help that I don't have to ask for. This type of help that can see the pain in my eyes because my chest is so heavy with the BS . . . yes, BS I have just experienced throughout my day at work, school, community, then off to my second hustle and third passion job. You know the professional woman grind. It's so exhausting, every single day. Sometimes, I don't have time to take care of myself. This is where that gyrlfriend comes into play.

The more I write, I understand, this sounds like a position for a fulltime job or intimate committed relationship, but it is a huge responsibility to be a gyrlfriend to me. But well worth it because I would do the same thing and more for you.

COLLEGE FRIEND-MINDED

Welcome to the college chronicles. I'm sure you have heard the phrase, "gyrls go to college to find a man and get married." Well, I didn't find either. I did find a bunch of gyrl roommates in Davidson Hall that were from all walks of life. As a college freshman at Hampton University, historically known for their high ratio of female to male school, I made a vow to make gyrlfriends and reinvent myself from the high nerd.

In high school I was known as the nerd and quiet choir gyrl, believe it or not. In college, I wanted to make a name for myself. I was heavily involved in campus activities, and I was extremely social. This afforded me a different social environment to accomplish my goal to make new gyrlfriends. My surroundings of gyrls increased, and I all of a sudden had more "so-called gyrlfriends" than true gyrlfriends. You know the kind that talk behind your back and try to steal your man. My plan backfired.

I never had a problem making friends, meaning friends would come to me. I never really went to other females and asked them to be my friend. I was extremely careful about who I let into my sista circle of friends. I am nice to everybody, but I have an unconscious vetting system that helps me assess gyrlfriends as designed sistas. I really do not know that I did it until now. This is probably because I am the only child and because I have a small, immediate family. Let's face it, as the only child, I had convinced myself that I my own best gyrlfriend. I often relied on myself. Can I get an Amen? Even if you are not the only child, women tend to operate this way.

FACT: We fail to realize our females in our family set up how we view other gyrlfriends.

PAUSE: You have to take a look at the women in your family in order to see where you got your sense of "gyrlfriendship."

GYRL, LISTEN!

The family-formation in your household plays a significant impact of how you interact with other females. This is where you first learned how you will interact with other females.

My grandmother was involved in several church groups and bowling groups. So the women in these groups would not only call her for business matters but for personal too. She was very direct and clear about keeping her boundaries with these groups of women. I learned at a young age not to mix business with personal matters. So my gyrlfriend groups that are business oriented are not usually personal

124

because if there is an incident that causes a rift, then it creates a mess that is difficult to clean up. Ultimately, I have to deal with these gyrlfriends in two different spaces, which can become exhausting to manage.

My mother, on the other hand, is a happy medium. She is involved in a sisterly social group that has created a merge of personal and professional. To the point where these women who are not blood are now my aunts. Yes . . . my aunts. Let's keep in mind my mother has no sisters. This is why I value my gyrlfriends like "sistas." I have watched my mom and my faux aunts' relationships evolve over time. No matter what came their way, they are there for each other.

THE EVOLUTION SAGA

I had just graduated from graduate school, and I was in a million pieces. I was dealing with the transitions of life. I was living with my parents and grandmother, seeking employment after completing my graduate degree, plus taking care of my mother who was diagnosed with cancer. So, to say the least, I had a lot on my plate. But I could not see it. Not to mention in a long-distance relationship that was not healthy. Yup, I said it. Not healthy for me at that time.

I am sure you're nodding your head right now. If not for the "Strong Black Woman Syndrome" but for the unhealthy relationships we often put ourselves in. Once again, I said it, "we put ourselves in."

125

Always remember we have choices in everything we do. It may not seem like it, but we do. We have decisions that require choices and the choice to make the decision. Simple but true.

In the midst of the storm, I was able to rely on my gyrlfriends. Some old, some new, but my gyrlfriends are who brought me through that storm. Trust me, there were many more storms to follow. My storm had cycles just like my gyrlfriends. My closest gyrlfriends made it through my college years all the way until now. They were aware of how I operate. Meaning, I would say, "I was okay," when I really was not. Then I would just burst out crying in the middle of dinner or just sitting around talking with them, and they would allow me to cry and talk about what I was holding in all at the same time.

Gyrl, you know, the "ugly cry" or catharsis, the cry where your throat closes up and you cannot swallow. Your chest starts to tighten, and before you know it, your eyes are closed, and tears are water falling down your face. Every thought you had been holding back has now come out in every tear drop. As the tears are running down your face, you do not think about where you are or who is looking at you. In that moment, you physically feel like your heart has broken into a million little pieces. You go to the sunken place where you cannot move.

I know when I open my eyes from crying I see my closest gyrlfriends looking at me with empathy because they have either gone through it, know someone else who has gone through it, or they feel

126

my pain as a gyrlfriend to gyrlfriend kind of love. My catharsis of emotions gives my problems a "face" of how hard this is for me to deal with. They allow me to cry, they do not ask questions, they validate their presence by saying "we are here," and they huddle around me. This may seem minor, but this is what works for me. Now think about what works for you. What do you need?

FACT: Crying is seen to some gyrlfriends as a sign of weakness. However, crying is a coping mechanism for the release of emotions: negative or positive.

PAUSE: The question is "Do you know what you need from your gyrlfriends?"

GYRL, LISTEN!

Only my closest gyrlfriends know how to deal with me when I get this way. How do your gyrlfriends help you through the tough times? Or are you always the one helping other gyrlfriends? Are you the "Strong" friend? What might that "Strong" gyrlfriend need from you?

FACT: As women, we project implicit bias on our gyrlfriends. This can cause "de" stress and isolation effecting unhealthy self-care practices.

PAUSE: The question is, "Do you pass judgement on your gyrlfriends who express their emotions (i.e. crying) outwardly in public or even in private gyrlfriend settings?"

GYRL, LISTEN!

I am sure you have had your fair share of gyrlfriends who have gotten this wrong. Yes, wrong. Let me give you an example. When you start crying, they say the following words: (1) Awww, I am sorry, (2) It's not your fault,. gyrl, (3) It's going to be okay, (4) It will be better, (5) It's okay let it out, or (6) Are you okay?

Gyrl, I know these may seem like "safe words," but do you really think your gyrlfriend wants to hear this during her "ugly cry?" As Black women, we have a term called the "ugly cry;" is a ritual that is done in private, often away from the public. The Black woman's construct has multiple layers, but the most pronounced is the "Strong Black Woman Syndrome." Yes, other cultures have stigma associated with women, and it is typically exploitative.

I understand that all women in some capacity are invisible, unheard, or taken advantage of. It is clear; we all have a fight to fight as women. The movement is a part of the collective initiation of being in a safe space with your gyrlfriends. You need a place where all the pieces of you are welcomed. Not judged, used, manipulated, and mistreated, just to name a few. My closest gyrlfriends gave me that through my catharsis circle. Gyrl, this sounds like music to my ears. What about you? Would you like to just "BE" with a group of women who you feel comfortable with? This was not only my safe space but theirs too.

SAFE GYRLFRIEND SPACE

If you are wondering what a catharsis circle is, it is not a cult. Well, maybe it is. No, gyrl, I am just joking. It was my safe haven to be my authentic self with gyrlfriends who saw me as vulnerable and raw as I was born into this world. I often wonder do other women have a support system similar to mine? Not that women have to do exactly what I do, but every woman should have another woman to turn to. I mean really turn to. To spill all her emotions, past or present, and sit and process or not with women who love you for you. This is what the catharsis process is.

The catharsis tradition known is loosely interpreted as a form of experiencing deep rooted emotions from the past that were repressed or ignored. The release of these emotions comes out due to them never having been adequately addressed at that time or fully experienced and resolved. When a catharsis happens, sometimes unplanned, especially if in public, it can be overwhelming for others. I have observed that initially a catharsis for a woman provides a "purification" and "purgation" ripple effect of emotions for other women around her. Think about when a woman cries, sometimes other women cry. Especially if they have a personal relationship.

WE ARE STRONGER TOGETHER

The various traumas that women experience are sometimes universal. The gender demographic bonds us like no other. Let's not forget the racial and cultural aspects of life. As women, we tend to turn our trauma into triumph. That is one thing we are good at doing, but reminder, we cannot do it alone.

The key is having a gyrlfriend around us to help us through the hard times and the good times. With the hope of stepping back to see all the pieces of the puzzle come together, hard times and all. All the million little pieces of you can be put together by the bonded glue of your gyrlfriends. This is why the relationship with your gyrlfriends needs to be strong and unwavering, like "gorilla glue!" No matter what, you have a strong bond that will stand the test of time. Not just the pop quizzes or midterm exams of life but the test that will shake you to your core. You need them more than you can even image. If you do not have a gyrlfriend or group of women, let me help you find them.

Gyrl, you might want to go warm up that tea you started sipping on and buckle up for safety. Life will go fast, and it might be a little bumpy, but reminder, you have a gyrlfriend driving this chapter. I vow to protect all the million little pieces of you because I love you like a S.I.S (Sista in Self-Care). I will show you the way. Let's ride!

NOW WHEN THE PIECES JUST FIT

Often relying on myself to get me through this storm, I now realize I need my closest gyrlfriends by my side. "My Three Musketeers," I named them "My Three Musketeers" because they would fight for me, even when I cannot fight for myself. I keep saying to myself, "gyrlfriends should not only be there to help you fight your external battles but your internal ones too."

Gyrl, you know what I mean, the internal conversation that you typically have with yourself throughout the day. I know I'm not the only one who has conversation in their head. Ten years ago, my conversation in my head was filled with self-doubt, self-hate, and self-destruction. My closest gyrlfriends helped me overcome those thoughts.

According to Webster, the definition of a gyrlfriend is a regular female companion or a woman's female friend with whom a relationship is formed (Merriam-Webster, 2018). This generic definition does not describe my set of gyrlfriends. If I could add a definition to Webster for my gyrlfriends, I would define them as (1) my circle, group, or tribe who consist of a focal point fixed to support, (2) my first responder designated or trained to respond to an emergency, (3) my life support who maintains my essential physical, emotional, spiritual, and mental functions when I am unhealthy, suffering, or in a toxic environment, (4) my natural agent that simulates sight and makes things visible, and (5) my extremely amazing and lighthearted laugh-a-thon pact. These five definitions are how I would describe my gyrlfriends. Gyrls, keep in mind these definitions are how I describe my gyrlfriends, so you cannot use these. I have already called Webster and begun the trademarking process for the release in 2019. Webster might put it in the urban volume of the dictionary series. We will see, stay tuned for the launch in the 2019 added words for dictionary definitions entitled "Not your gyrlfriend's urban dictionary."

All jokes aside, I know this sounds like a well-rounded definition of what every gyrlfriend should be, plus or minus other definitions, but my definition took me a long time to develop. Similar to the evolution of myself.

My Three Musketeers would just pop up out of the blue to rescue me from others or myself. Okay, maybe not out of the blue, but they all have shown themselves true to help me when I needed them the most. My gyrlfriends often tell me the things I don't want to hear but need to. They all take care of me beyond my mind, body, and soul.

Most of the time, I did not have to ask for help because they can hear it in my voice. Which is important: if you know me, I do not like to ask for help. I am unlearning some of the "strong" woman ways of life because they can only get me so far in life.

I am aware that I am a work in progress toward the process of the best version of me. I can say I have all three of my sistas on this committed journey of growth.

Teresa Suber Goodman

Co-Author

Moving a lot when younger, Teresa experienced subsequent challenges of forging and maintaining friendships that could endure the test of time. Subsequently, she learned to adapt when necessary. Her experiences will help us identify why some relationships fail to last and why some with great potential, will only exist in a superficial manner.

The Adaptation Code
From Inside Looking Out

I am definitely a product of my environment. All that I have seen heard, and more importantly, experienced have shaped my best and worst relationships, my fears, and guided the decisions I've made regarding my gyrlfriends.

Growing up, the original examples of relationships that I saw belonged to my family. Be the relationships good or bad, they served as my introduction of how to choose my friends, treat my friends, and keep my friends, and they all came from those I loved the most.

My first prerequisite for making friends was that they had to be a part of my family. This limited the number of friends I had and limited the experiences that would potentially teach me how to develop healthy friendships. For you see, there were several obstacles that I ran into.

First, because my friendships were limited to those in my family, I had few skills when it came to actually making friends. Second, we moved several times, and that affected my friendships as well. Lastly, during my formative years, I never witnessed women in dedicated friendships with a close gyrlfriend.

I didn't know how to introduce myself or share my thoughts and feelings with someone outside of my family unit. An only child for almost ten years, I learned to play alone and entertain myself without having to take into consideration the needs or wants of others. I mimicked what I saw around me, so I didn't make an effort to develop outside friendships. Often, I still find myself retreating into the comfort zone in my head where I think things through, and regularly, I entertain myself with my thoughts. I'm brazen and such a go-getter in my headspace; my comfort lies in understanding that I'm not at risk of rejection, being misunderstood, or ridiculed, which makes it a safe place. The problem is that space isn't inviting or nurturing to anyone other than myself.

I remember briefly having neighbors that were about my age; three children who lived next door, two gyrls and a boy, all very close to my age. Sometimes, I would look out of the window and long to play with them, but I was too afraid and didn't know how to interject myself into the group. Finally, getting up the nerve (I do not recollect how I introduced myself or if they introduced themselves to me), I remember playing together and having a great time. Unfortunately, we moved before I could develop a genuine relationship with those neighbors.

Each time we moved, I developed surface or superficial relationships with gyrls but never got to develop a deep, lasting relationship with a true gyrlfriend that I could carry into adulthood.

After moving and leaving friends several times, I started learning how to make 'right now' friends so that I wouldn't be hurt by losing them if I had to leave. Sometimes, I lost friendships because I wasn't sure what to do to keep them. Do I call or write (people still wrote letters when I grew up . . . we used pay phones, didn't have cable or internet, and television went off at midnight), do I make a joke, or just start talking? I had no idea how to develop or maintain relations with friends.

I honestly believe these practices led me to handicap myself early on when it came to making and developing friendships with women who could have potentially been my best gyrlfriends.

In high school, I learned to be social, to laugh, carry on conversations, and be interested in the things that were popular during those days and times. I developed friendships that weren't necessarily good for me as we did not have similar interests, but I "went along to get along." As I got to know myself better in the years to come, I wished I had found friends who I had more in common with and who I shared similar interests with. I also regret not maintaining relationships with my gyrlfriends for longer than a few months or, at best, a year when I moved.

Heading into college, I made a conscious decision that the past was behind me. I was excited that I now had a chance to make friends on my own terms. During my college years and the years following, I honestly did meet some of the best friends I'd ever have, but it's also the time I made some of the biggest mistakes I'd ever make that ended up costing me some of these friendships.

Somewhere along the way, I developed a 'right now' friendship theory. I believe this was because, when we moved, I had mastered the ability to formulate superficial relationships that I learned to put aside once we were no longer in the same place at the same time. I learned this behavior as a result of moving away from those I cared about. That theory did not serve me well because the people on the other side were cut off, and I limited my own chance at cultivating potentially deep friendships.

My only lasting relationships were with family; there were hiccups in those as well, but we pressed forward because we were going to be together no matter what. To this day, my longest, most enduring friendship is with one of my cousins who is my age; we were born less than a month apart, and we know where each other's secrets are buried, and I know she will take my confidence to the grave as I will hers. We've had stumbling blocks, but we made it through the storms one way or another.

I was also a toxic gyrlfriend because the surface relationships I'd developed did not allow me to grow as a good, dependable friend. Fortunately, I found a few friends who showed me what true friendship was all about through their actions and their words. These women did not judge me but modeled what friendship is made of, and they loved me through my inabilities as I played catch-up.

I developed one particular relationship that began as I met and connected with a co-worker, where I finally opened myself up and was the most honest and forthcoming in a non-familial friendship that I had ever been. I was honest and let myself be myself, and when I did something she didn't like, she iced me out of her life and taught me important lessons that helped me grow tremendously. I remember it like yesterday, and I can feel the shame and the pain like it is fresh (the saying 'people never forget how you made them feel' is absolutely true).

We'd gone out of town, and at some point during the tail end of the trip, I said something that she didn't like. She was a little sharp with me, and I automatically withdrew and accepted the guilt of being wrong. The more I thought of it, I was convinced I wasn't wrong this time. I spoke to another person I thought was a friend in my anger and challenged if my former friend was right.

I thought I was in a safe space, but I learned later that not only did she tell some of what I said, but she also didn't tell the entire story and attributed some things to my commentary that I clearly stated were told to me. Boy was I mad; I mean, I was livid. So I lost two friends and was very angry because I felt unprotected and unjustly accused. It took more than a year, but I was finally able to move on, although the hurt was still there.

I learned that the healing was mine to have only if I was willing to move forward past the wrongs and, most importantly, the hurt. I learned to let the anger go and continue forward because I'd grown when it came to my gyrlfriends, and I chose to heal myself rather than continue to be a surface friend. I put the 'right now' theory away and confronted my weaknesses head on.

I started to ask myself the following questions: *Why did I have a lack of trust with my gyrlfriends? Why was it so hard to connect with other women?*

My answer was simple and went back to watching my neighbors play as I looked out the window: I was afraid of not being accepted and liked for who I truly am. Confronting the truth that held me back from being a good gyrlfriend and for making good gyrlfriends was a hard pill to swallow, but I learned so very much as I worked through my insecurities. Because I was often a toxic gyrlfriend, I knew how to identify them and some of the steps to heal from it as well.

How to recognize a toxic friendship:

1. You feel lonely when she is there.
2. You only share certain things with them to limit criticism or judgement.
3. Everything has to be one person's way all the time. Things can't always be about you.

4. Decisions are made that serve the purpose of one individual more than the other. Selfish decisions are dangerous. No one benefits from getting their way all the time.

5. You're punished when you do or say something they don't like, cutting off communication and support when the other party offered a differing opinion/action.

6. When you can't recall any intimate details about your gyrlfriend, but she may know all of yours. It's more than likely she was only a surface friend.

7. When there is no evidence of growth. No one is becoming their best self as a result of this relationship.

8. When trouble strikes, you don't go to this person without hesitation or fear of judgement. If you have to second-guess their ability or willingness to support you, there is a problem.

9. If the friend hasn't come to grips with their own issues while continually pointing out where you could be better.

There is a risk you take when you are vulnerable enough to share your thoughts and feelings with those you trust. True gyrlfriends will protect those vulnerabilities and help you navigate and be your best self. I've been blessed to learn the hallmarks of healthy friendships as a result of my journey.

How to recognize (and be) a good gyrlfriend:

1. She is honest with you, even with delicate subjects.
2. She doesn't stay mad and doesn't allow you to either.
3. She supports your healthy choices, even when it's not in her best interest.
4. She takes you into consideration and compromises with you.
5. You can be transparent with no judgement from her.
6. She doesn't use your past mistakes against you.
7. When trouble strikes, she's there, no questions.
8. She shares her life with you as she expects you to do with her.

E. Che'meen Johnson
Co-Author

E. Che'meen wants to help you explore the levels of friendship and set some ground rules. We use the word "friend" far too often for everyone we know, which can be problematic and lead to misunderstandings.

The Hierarchy Code
There are Levels to Gyrlfriendship

When I think of Gyrlfriend Code, I think of the different levels of friendships I have and the different levels of expectation I have for each. Yep, yep, there are levels to gyrlfriendship. When things are going good in your friendships, there are joyful exchanges that add to your life fulfillment. However, when things aren't going well, now that's when things get tricky.

I have found that the clearer I am on my priorities, the easier it is for me to establish what level my friendships are at with this gyrlfriend and the appropriate gyrlcode that should be expected or used. To be totally honest, when it comes to friendship, I'm usually not the one to leave that relationship. I am usually that friend you feel you have outgrown or, in some cases, out used. I understand that like most people, gyrlfriends are in your life for a reason, season or lifetime. And like most things, only time will tell. As I have seasoned in life, I have learned to handle those gyrlfriend departures with grace, knowing that my greater good requires that you no longer be part of my life experience. That's my higher conscience's way of saying "kick rocks, I'm good." It wasn't always like that, but thank the LAWD for growth and maturity.

Firstly, I am an admitted Recovering Drama Queen. Today, I can admit my recovery proudly. Knowing what my addiction is and how it works directly corresponds to why I usually don't leave friendships. I love being part of all my gyrlfriends' levels of drama. I will ride shotgun to most anybody else's drama any damn day. A long time ago, I gave up the concept of having one best friend. I needed a squad to handle all of me. If I'm Oprah, there will be many Gayles. I even broke them down, what they bring to my life, just in case they need to be replaced. But first, let's discuss the different levels of friendship. Then we will discuss the different types of friends. Usually, we consider someone a friend at the Close and Intimate Levels.

LEVELS OF INVOLVEMENT

Acquaintances Level: We know each other and don't have any issues. You can share a basic conversation and laugh. From what you can tell, they're okay.

Gyrlfriend Code:

-You greet them when you see them.

Casual Level: We know each other, have had a few conversations or laughs on the latest celebrity gossip, state of the world, or the situation at hand. We have been in each other's presence with no issues. Usually, there is some reason for yawl (you all) to be around each other. You have been around them enough to have established some sort of rapport. You generally have a good opinion of them.

146

Gyrlfriend Code:

-When you see each other, you exchange pleasantries.

Close Level: We're cool with each other. We are friends, we have similar interests or something in common, and invest time in each other. We know each other's family dynamics and background. We may even share other mutual friends. We hang out and share life experiences. You usually give this person an overview of what's going on but don't give them all the intimate details, unless they have experience on the subject matter. Usually, this is a person you have almost daily contact with. Yawl support each other through the day-to-day stuff.

Gyrlfriend Code:

-When sharing another friend's personal business, we don't use their name.

-We don't judge each other per se but do pass judgement for our own lives.

-We can agree to disagree and still be cool.

Intimate Level: These are your ride or die friends. Usually, they are long term friends but not always. You may or may not see or speak to each other every day or even often, but when you do, it's like nothing has changed. At this level, yawl consider each other family. You have supported each other through some major life events. This person knows you; they know the good, bad, the ugly, and the truth. An intimate relationship is where time and emotions have been invested on both of your parts. We have an agreement either spoken or unspoken that we are going to be there for each other. Our bullsh*t is compatible, and we can share who we really are unmasked. I can tell you all the details of what is going on in my life, name dropping along the way, in these intimate relationships. You usually feel comfortable with sharing who you are and being vulnerable. Isn't that what it's all about, allowing yourself to be vulnerable? I don't know about you, but I have been Captain Save-A-Hoe on too many occasions. Guess what, Captain Save-A-Hoe needs a Captain Save-A-Hoe too.

It's usually when these close or intimate relationships go awry that we experience hurt. The last thing you expect is for your gyrlfriend in your close or intimate circle to do you wrong. It usually hurts on many levels because this person knows you. At this point, you should know each other enough to know what yawl don't or shouldn't do. At higher involvement levels, there are expectations of respect and honesty that are written into your friendship. Note: gyrlfriends should be extended the same "benefit of the doubt" that you give your man.

By this time, we should have established a certain way in which we operate. You should each know what the other stands for. We should know what communication style works best for us. There should be somewhat clear boundaries that are never to be crossed. You should know what is acceptable and unacceptable to do around the other person. If your gyrlfriend doesn't smoke but you do, you may choose to refrain from smoking or choose to step away from her to take a smoke break. She in turn, would know not to come to where you are smoking and subsequently complain about the smoke.

In a friendship, you learn about the person and try to respect how they do things. You also need to communicate when offensive things happen. The way I determine my close level friends from intimate level friends is by how we handle conflict. If we can have that hard conversation, but love, trust, and respect are still present, then that gyrlfriendship is at the highest level. Now, if we reach the highest level of gyrlfriendship and you knowingly do something that hurts me without communication first, our season of friendship is over. If you know I am not going to like something but feel strongly that you must do this thing, there may be a slight chance we can continue to be friends only after I disclose my feelings on the subject.

There are just some things that fall into the "I am informing you of my decision only because we are friends" category, but I'm a grown a** woman, so "it is what it is." When a gyrlfriend approaches you like that, respect needs to be given. Now, if said person does something that knowingly hurts you but decides to tell you after the fact, that's when I say "f*ck 'um," they have broken gyrlfriend code, period! Technically, they have already said the same to you by not showing their respect in telling you in advance. I will leave you with this, cherish your close and intimate relationships. You are blessed to have them, so don't take them for granted. Women in gyrlfriendships are a beautiful thing!

Gyrlfriend Code:

- You tell the truth completely, admitting the wrong you did.

- If I do speak the business and name of another of my friends, you are sworn to secrecy

-If you or they inadvertently caused someone's feeling to be hurt, start the conversation off with "I f**ked up."

-If you find yourself all in your feelings being "extra," admit it.

FRIEND TYPES

<u>Praying friends</u> – This friend has Jesus on the mainline; you probably will refrain from overuse of profanity around them. You can bear witness to seeing, knowing they are either praying or fasting for something or someone and God moving on their behalf. You know when you asked them to pray for you, you are good and covered no matter how things work out. Whatever happens is either God sent or God used for your good. You may be squinting on the issue now, but ultimately, it will be great or a lesson learned. You know Jesus got her back and got your back too (no, church attendance isn't required). Now, this person doesn't necessarily need to be a Christian; they can be spiritually plugged into the Universal Good. Either way, they have the hook up to the comfort you need presently.

Gyrlfriend Code:

-You are in need of HELP, are ready to surrender your ego, and be honest, just ask.

Ratchet friend – Now this is a friend that will tell and show you how to get down and not do jail time for the petty, low-road thinking or activities at hand. This is that friend that will go with you to slash your cheating boyfriend's tires and let you know you're only supposed to slash three tires if he got full-coverage car insurance (four slashed tires is considered an anomaly and covered). This sister has the black Special Ops suit in the back of the closet in case of emergencies because "you never know." I believe everybody should have a friend like this in their circle. Even if they just remind you that you are better than that. That friend that can peep game a mile away and can think like a dude. Someone who asks for advice saying, "I'm asking for a friend." When you find yourself d*ckmatized or being petty, this friend doesn't pass judgement; they understand the craziness of it all.

Gyrlfriend Code:
-Be honest about your level of crazy, and speak to another friend before you take any action.

Higher Consciences Friend: This friend is the one you need to talk you off the ledge. This friend knows you and can say things in such a way that you feel empowered to come up to a higher level of thinking. They can just hit you with commonsense in a way you can accept. Now in this category, you may have several friends that use different approaches to talk you down, out, or whatever is needed to get you back in the right mindset. There is the "Straight No Chaser" approach. This usually contains profanity and can feel like a slap in the face.

{Example: Chick, if you don't stop with the BS and sit your ass down.} Another approach may appeal more to how far you have come, showing your growth and maturity. {Example: Chick, you are better than this, you're/we are too grown for THIS.} Then there is the praying/spiritual approach. {Example: You should be or show love.} Depending on what is going on and who you are talking to, one or more of these approaches may be used.

Gyrlfriend Code:

-Just know that however they are saying it, it is out of love.

-Be open to listening.

-Surrender your ego.

Drama Queen Friend: Most us have at least one of these friends or a family member like this. This gyrlfriend is usually over the top, honest, and very funny. You either accept them for who they are or just leave them alone. Drama Queens (DQs) are known for being somewhat loud, overbearing, and highly opinionated. As a Recovering Drama Queen, I always saw being a Drama Queen as a gift; it's like having a superpower. The sheer boldness of personality, an unwillingness to dull your light for those that aren't comfortable with your shining. I feel it deserves an applause. Do realize that no matter what you do, some people will never be comfortable with a bold personality. DQs are expressive when talking; they can be a full cast of characters all while telling a single story. Let me also note that most DQs are more annoyed than mad about most things. Usually, if you are convicted about who you really are and stand in your skin, most DQs will respect you. Most DQs are usually good at discerning a situation, then bold enough to say what everyone is thinking but doesn't want to say. Please note: not all Drama Queens are loud and out front bold. There are undercover DQs who usually do their work covertly in the background. They still shine bright, but they are more selective of the group of people they shine for.

Gyrlfriend Code:
-If something upsets you about something a DQ said, let them know; it probably wasn't done in malice.
-Don't discount the message because of the way message was given.

<u>Drama Vampire Friend</u>: This gyrlfriend usually is only in your life for a season or reason. They don't usually stand the test of time because after they have bled you dry emotionally, they moved on to the next person. This is the gyrlfriend who always seems to have something "cray-cray" going on in their life. These gyrlfriends most often come from the Casual and Acquaintance level of friendships and are quick to rise through the ranks because they reach out to you constantly and consistently.

They will tell you all about the terrible things going on in their life, and if they believe they have a sympathetic ear, they will hook you into their life of drama. This type of person will cling to whoever will listen without passing too much judgement. For me, this was truly never an

153

issue; it helped feed my addiction nicely. I got a chance to experience full drama without it truly affecting any major aspect of my life. It wasn't until recent that I realized the drama was actually taking an emotional toll on me.

I used to enjoy the daily hit about how unfair life was for the other party. I used to eat up what I was being told as tasty morsels. However, when bad choices could lead to something as dire as homelessness, I would get worried. Not so much for my friend but for their children. As a third-generation property owner/manager, who also managed Single Residency Housing, I know that not having housing stability can send a person's world into a tailspin. Being homeless with children takes me out of my "judging NOT judging gyrlfriend mode" into "concerned nurturer gyrlfriend mode," who can seem more judgmental than caring. Plus, by this time. I would be on too many roller coaster scenarios to NOT conclude that this gyrlfriend is an emotional Drama Vampire sucking the all the goodwill and kindness out of me.
Gyrlfriend Code:
-Know thy self, enough to know when it's time to pull back or jump ship.
-Your self-care comes first.

Relationships amongst gyrlfriends can sometimes be as complicating as they are fulfilling. The beautiful thing is YOU always have a choice about who and what you allow in your life. What I have learned over the years is the better friend I am to myself, the better friend I can be to other women. Also, when my priorities are in order, choosing the right gyrlfriends for my life situations isn't difficult.

Everything in life is a lesson! The tool that has helped me the most is journaling. Recording my life has been a saving grace. I can write what I truly feel without edit or fear of repercussion. By now, we should all know that what you say matters. No one has to know all the "not so nice" thoughts that circle within your mind. Journaling has also allowed me to fully account for events that transpired months earlier with clarity in wording and motive. {My ex-boyfriend was shook when I whipped out my journal and read the full details of his indiscretions. It also came in handy when a former friend tried to recant her story to avoid appearing like a snake.} My trusty journal captured everything. Some of my greatest lessons have been: Trust your instincts! If you witness a friend doing another one of their friends dirty, it's just a matter of time before they will do the same to you! When someone says they don't want to be judged, they have already judged! You may rank one of your friends at a higher level of involvement than they rank you; don't be mad! F*ckery usually proceeds a breakdown in communication and the relationship.

Ashley Little

Co-Author

Ashley helps us understand when seasons are over and when friendships have served their purposes in our lives. Seasons bring blessings and lessons. Although the friendships may end, lessons are life-long.

The Seasonal Code
Seasons of Friendship

People come into our lives for a reason, a season, or a lifetime. Throughout the years, I had to learn and grow in this area. I didn't always understand the difference between a seasonal friend and a lifetime friend. Loyalty is very important to me in all of my relationships. I believe in supporting and being there for my friends. However, I have encountered seasons where I thought I lost friendships, but the reality was the friendship was only for a season. Going through those seasons were very uncomfortable for me. I didn't understand why some people I was holding onto were falling off, not realizing at the time that they were only there for a season.

First, people come into our lives for a REASON; it is usually to meet a need. Most of the time, they are there to help you through a difficult time in your life. They are there for guidance and support to aid you physically, emotionally, or spiritually. When the assignment is up, they will leave without any wrongdoing on your part. Throughout my life, I have had colleagues, friends, and family members who were in my life for a reason. Sometimes, when we are going through difficult times in our lives, God will send people to help us. I have had colleagues who I thought would be life-long friends who came into my life to help me through some of the hardest times in my career.

Learning later that everything was necessary, and it was a reason why they were sent to help me.

When I first moved to Virginia Beach, VA, I went through a season of unhappiness with the company I was working with. During that time, I had a colleague who I was very close to who help me get through it. Our friendship grew, and I thought it was going to be a life-long friendship. In actuality, her role was never positioned to be that of a life-long friend. She was sent to teach me patience and to motivate me to keep going no matter the storm.

God uses people to push you into your destiny. Even though I was unhappy in my "Now Season," she was positioned to prepare me for my "Next Season." Our friendship ended after I relocated for my promotion within the company. When our friendship ended, I didn't understand how we lost communication.

I had to learn to reflect and be thankful for the season. It is okay when people leave that are not meant to continue with you on your journey. God sent her in my life during that time to help me get to the next level in my career. If God did not position the divine connection into my life during that difficult time, I would have left the company and missed my promotion.

When we go through different trials and tribulations in our lives, it's a painful process, and we have to ask God to send divine connections and position the right people in our lives to help us get to the next level. Our destiny is tied to our connections.

Gyrlfriend, when people come into our lives for a SEASON, it is our turn to share, grow, or learn. They may bring you laughter and peace. They may teach you something new. They may give you a great amount of joy. Believe it! It is real!! It is only for a season. Once you understand this process, letting go will be much easier. I had to go through this process a couple of times in order for me to truly accept it and understand it.

I had gyrlfriends who I grew up with who are no longer in my circle of friends. The friendships were fun and exciting, and life was good. August 2004, we left for college, and our lives started to change. We attended different colleges, but we all came back together during different events and for the holidays. Attending different colleges allowed us to grow and experience new things. As we continued to evolve in our lives, we noticed our lives were changing in many different areas . . . babies, marriages, new circles, and different goals and mindsets. During that time, I was very uncomfortable because I didn't want to accept the friendships were coming to an end. I tried to hold on to some of them, but it was beginning to become toxic.

When we try to hold on to things that God wants us to let go of, we are delaying our destiny. I was bothered for a while, but as time passed, things became clearer to me. I had to realize we were all in different places in our lives. We were growing apart and it was okay—life does not always go as planned.

Gyrlfriend, we have to be okay with letting people go when they walk away. We have to learn to embrace and trust the process. I know it hurts, and sometimes, it's hard to accept. The process is necessary, and it is not a negative thing. Reflect on the reason why that person was in your life and what you learned.

Life experiences, as you continue to grow and evolve, have a way of waking you up. I really didn't understand seasons of friendships until I faced challenges and storms in some of my own friendships. Those moments exposed the reason why they were in my life and why the friendship could not continue. True friends will be by your side cheering you on through every achievement, regular day, or trial you face in life.

Gyrlfriend, you do not have to be angry when people reveal themselves; instead, embrace it and thank God for blocking it.

I'm an extrovert, so making friends and meeting new people comes natural to me. I had to learn that friendships shift and change through time. Sometimes, God sends people into your life to help you get through different moments. Friendships come and go, and it truly is a fact of life, but at the end of the day, if someone does not want to be in your life, you're truly better off without them.

Lastly, life will teach you who your life-long friends are. I was very frustrated and bothered when some people I trusted became strangers. Instead of me making it about the season, I made it about me and them. There are some seasons where we have to understand the position people play in our life and vice versa. We want them to be our best friend, but they are only there for the moment. Maybe that's not supposed to be your circle of friends, and that's okay.

Lifetime friends are people you are comfortable with even after you have been separated. Gyrlfriend, a lifetime friend is someone you are going to have an instant connection with, and they are friends who turn into family. As you continue to grow and elevate, your circle will get smaller. However, the friends who are meant to be there for a lifetime are not going to go anywhere. I have a few lifetime gyrlfriends who have been with me through the good times and the bad times. I know these ladies are my lifetime friends because even when we are apart, we can pick back up where we left off. We have our disagreements, but we always find a way to come to a middle ground. We support, celebrate, laugh, and cry together.

It hurts to grow apart from people who were once important to you. At the end of the day, you have to cherish the people who choose to stick by your side. A lifetime friendship is a friendship that has been tested by time and still stands strong. It will stay in your heart and never be erased. Gyrlfriend, take care of the people who show you a friendship that lasts a lifetime. Real friends who appreciate you and consider you as their best friend will always find a way.

Nobody wants to go through different emotions of rejection, abandonment, or betrayal, but we have to look to God to heal those wounds. It's a painful process when you have built strong connections with people, but you have to forgive and move on. Friendships should not define us; they should refine us. Continue to trust God and identify yourself with His truths and ask Him for guidance, He will never leave you. Embrace your current season and the people who are in it.

Friendships are not easy to keep forever; they are going to challenge your patience, understanding, and your sympathy. Gyrlfriend, it's important to keep friends in your life that will have your back through the good and the bad. Always welcome new friendships and understand everyone is not meant to be a lifetime friend.

Brittaney Nicole Pleasant
Co-Author

Brittaney depicts how jealousy, a natural human emotion, can creep into friendships. What happens when one person in the relationship succeeds and the other does not? What do you do when the support you expect to receive is not extended? We need to not only look outwards but also inwards on our journey towards self-love. The key here is looking within.

The Self-Reflection Code
Jealous Much?

Do you ever get jealous of your gyrlfriend? Can you genuinely celebrate her, even when it seems like your world is being turned upside down? At some point in our relationships with our gyrlfriends, we may have all had different answers to these questions. I know I have. Whether you're the gyrlfriend that is always positive and supportive no matter what, or whether you've caught yourself becoming distant or secretly giving your gyrlfriend an eyeroll or side eye when she calls to tell you good news, jealousy in our relationships with our gyrlfriends is something we definitely need to discuss. Here's my story.

I had a gyrlfriend that we'll call Zoe. Zoe and I were from two completely different backgrounds. I've always been extremely shy and introverted unless I'm close to you (then you probably wish I would shut up). Zoe was an extrovert with a loud, in your face, take it or leave it type of personality. Still, we shared similarities that caused us to click the first day we met. I think the coolest thing, and probably the thing that really helped us to bond, was the fact that we were dating guys from the same family. My boyfriend at the time was the uncle to her boyfriend. Of course, we had tons of gyrl talk about how cool it would be to marry into the family together and have children, etc. We had it all figured out, but there were a couple of things life had in store that we didn't quite consider. One of those things was age difference. Zoe and I were the same age, but our boyfriends were different ages. My boyfriend was older, 27 and her boyfriend was younger, 22. With age comes maturity (sometimes). Even though my boyfriend was only 27, he was ready to settle down, and so was I, so one year after we started dating (and after finding out I was pregnant), we got married. This is where things started to go left with my friendship with Zoe.

Everything was wonderful with my marriage for the most part at first, but after the birth of our son, we definitely had those days where happily ever after just didn't seem to exist. There was cheating, lies, late nights when I would be home alone until 2 and 3 in the morning while I was pregnant, etc. On those days, I was so glad I could call and vent or cry to Zoe. Her advice seemed sound and reasonable at the time, but I didn't realize the seeds that were being planted. She was going through her own problems in her relationship, and I was her shoulder to lean on as well. Slowly, I started noticing a change in Zoe. My husband and I had fallen out of love (and even like) with each other for a while, but we fought through it like many married couples who decided being with each other was more important than parting ways and being without each other. Now, you would think your best friend would be happy for you, right? I mean, she would always tell me she was, but her actions toward me started to change.

When she would call and ask me how me and my husband were doing, and I would say "good," she would cut the conversation short, and I wouldn't hear from her for a couple of days. On the other hand, if I called when my husband and I weren't getting along very well, things would be like they used to. We would talk and I would go over to her house and we would chill like old times.

I noticed the change, but it didn't really start to bother me until I stopped being invited to go different places, and it seemed I only got a phone call when she needed something. Even then, Zoe was more distant than she had ever been. There were social media posts with pictures of her and her other "besties," and we barely talked at times because she was always "tired." One day, I just decided to ask what was wrong. Why things weren't the way they used to be between us, and her response was, "Well, I just feel like you changed from the day you said 'I do.' I quit calling you about my problems with Sean because you're married. You don't understand what I'm going through." Now, I'm not totally insensitive to how she was feeling, but I honestly got angry, and I felt extremely hurt. Even though things didn't turn out how we planned as far as both of us getting married, I never changed and didn't feel that I should have been treated differently. Eventually, we stopped talking altogether for other reasons, but the jealousy was there and evident all along.

So let me ask you, why do we allow jealousy to come between our friendships? In my situation, I never once felt like I was better than Zoe or treated her any different from when we first met. If anything, I bent over backwards, even lying at times or not disclosing how well things were going for me so that when things weren't going well in her relationship or her life, she wouldn't feel out of place. In many situations, things like this don't seem to matter. In my opinion, we as women have to be careful that our emotions don't get in the way of our blessings. I feel that the friends, the true friends and even the ones that were not so true, are blessings in our lives. We can learn from each other no matter what stage of life we are in if we would only allow it to happen.

Advice To My Gyrls:

Love yourself so much that you never even feel the need to be jealous of another woman. You see, so many things can be avoided if we just learn to truly love ourselves. We all go through different seasons and experiences in life that are unique to our journey. It's not always going to be rose petals and rainbows, and we have to be okay with that because on the other side of the storm, we come out stronger and more beautiful than ever before.

My favorite flower is the lotus flower. Think of yourself as this flower. It grows in the murky, muddy waters, but when it has reached maturity and blooms on top of the water, its petals are free of the mud and debris that it had to go through to grow. You may not have had what you consider the best life. There will be moments where you feel like you're smothering, drowning in the mud. There are days when you may feel ugly and worthless. There will always be someone who may be further in life than you. There will always be someone who may drive a better car or dress better than you, but if you really think about it, it's a matter of perspective.

Gyrls, my Queens, stop looking to the left or to the right of you. Look within yourself and learn to appreciate yourself and each part of your journey. Yes, the process maybe hard at times, but everything you go through is necessary to help you become the woman that you were created to be. So give yourself time to bloom like the lotus flower, and along the way, embrace the women that may cross your path. You never know what the next woman may have been through that can help you get to your next level. You also may never know how you can help the next woman. Just because another woman looks like she has it all together, she could be crumbling on the inside. We all carry our burdens differently. Be kind, always, and never let your insecurities shine brighter than your beauty.

Ariel V. Dixon

Co-Author

Ariel's "Death of the Instant Bestie," depicts what happens when labeling is conducted hastily without really taking a look at the fibers, fabric, and intrinsic value of the relationship.

The Labeling Code
The Tragedy of The Instant Bestie

I am the oldest of four children. This status defines me. It is the basis for most of my personality traits, both good and bad. I was only on this planet for two years as a solo act. From the age of two, I have had at least one best friend. My three siblings and I are freakishly clickish. We don't require outsiders because we have each other. This reliance on my family-besties began in my formative years following a discussion with a most likely inebriated favorite aunt who pulled me aside and said something akin to, "I don't mess with b%$#hes." This was not an angry exclamation but rather a calm statement laced with Absolute and cranberry juice. If I recall, this conversation took place during a defining time in my life—seventh grade. What I gathered from our exchange, at the tender age of 13, was that gyrls are messy.

Think back to middle school/junior high. Everyone is awkward and insecure, so we band together. There is protection in the pack. The problem with banding together is that groups of gyrls are rarely happy just being a group of gyrls. There has to be some kind of drama. You like a boy that gyrl likes, so now y'all hate each other. That gyrl doesn't have the latest Girbaud jeans (1996 . . . I'm saying) and she wears her hair like that . . . we don't talk to her. "You talk like a white gyrl . . . you think you're better than everybody else?"

Many of us survived these years to become better people; however, a few of us are still stuck (mentally) in junior high. And if gyrls are messy, women can be down-right vicious. For this reason, as I grew up, I remembered the sentiment of my auntie, and my sisters became my true best friends. Over the years, God blessed me with genuine additions to my personal sisterhood. It takes time to build a true friendship; and my Gyrlfriends, the ones that really show up and stick around, have been cultivated over years.

There was a brief period of time during which the label of "friend" extended past my carefully developed relationships. I call this period of time my Second Childhood (thank you, Nas).

I entered my Second Childhood in 2009, when I enrolled in law school to pursue a juris doctorate degree. Typical tales of law school survival are replete with sleepless nights in the library, mental breakdown, and fatigue. This was definitely a part of my law school experience, but for the most part, law school for me was like a second shot at an undergraduate experience (I was very tame in college). I spent most nights of the week during law school at various bars, lounges, and house parties. My social calendar was never-ending and as I stretched my party wings, I picked up new gyrlfriends. We established our friendships with shots, cocktails, Spades, and the Wobble.[1] All it took was a text

---

[1] Disclaimer: If you are contemplating a law school experience, this is not the norm. Do not attempt this rock-star lifestyle at home . . . You might not make it.

message or a quick phone call and the good time was poppin. "Hey Gyrl, we are meeting at (insert desired bar here) at 10." "How we steppin? Grown-folks classy or freak 'em dress?"

That conversation was all it took. I would be in the streets until it was time for most people to start waking up and preparing for their day (again, I stress, this life is not for amateurs). These excursions were supported by several gyrlfriends—most of whom were not attending law school. One in particular was always ready to go. We met at a house party, and she was introduced as the gyrlfriend of a mutual guy-friend. We instantly made a gyrlfriend-esk connection. We will call her Sasha (that seems fitting).

Sasha was instantly identifiable as a "fun person." She loved to dance, drank like an Asgardian, and had an extremely likeable, if not lovable, personality. Sasha was the kind of "friend" that was always willing to drop whatever she was doing to meet you for whatever reason. We would talk almost every day and went out most nights of the week. Sasha and I, along with other members of this tribe, would rarely be seen out without each other. If I was there, Sasha and the other gyrls weren't far behind and vice versa. This relationship was attractive at that point in my life as I, and my other gyrlfriends of that era, were always looking for the next party. The warning signs that this might be a toxic relationship just were not visible to me, although others outside of our circle could see the "Danger, Will Robinson!" lights flashing.

This relationship persisted in this way until about my third year of law school. Just for context, up until my third and final year of law school, I was readily available for most, if not all, social engagements. During my third year, a lot of things happened to cause me to pull back; the first event being the death of my grandmother. My gyrls were all there for me the best way they could be, given the fact that I didn't really share the heartbreak openly. Following the passing of my grandmother, I calmed down significantly; in addition, it was during this final year of school that I really began to take an active role in law school related responsibilities. With finals, extracurricular academic engagements, a new boo thang, and the dreaded bar exam looming, I fell back from the nightlife scene.

All of my gyrls, and guys for that matter, were very supportive through my graduation and my bar prep.[2] I successfully sat for the bar that summer and began my transition from law student to lawyer. As my focus changed and my social interests began to evolve, my desire to be out in the social scene changed. Thus began the true decline of my relationship with Sasha. Our once carefree and mimosa-filled association spiraled from, "That's my gyrl!" to, "That bish is THROWED!" Loyalty, loyalty, loyalty. This is where we get caught up. Ride or die. Through thick and thin. Besties forever. All of these phrases, just like when we apply them to our romantic situations, make it seem as though, no matter what, a gyrlfriend should be down for the cause. This rings even more

---

[2] This is where your soul shrivels and dies as you attempt to cram the entire legal history of a state into your brain. I still have nightmares.

true for a "best friend." But what if you haven't signed up to be a "best friend?"

It is amazing to meet another female with whom you instantly "click" as an adult. As we mature in mentality and age, it becomes difficult to find our tribe—to discern who is truly present for mutual betterment, and who is just trying to get over. There is a joy that comes from meeting a potential gyrlfriend.

When Sasha and I were first introduced, we sat and chatted for at least an hour. Music in the background, drinks in hand, we bantered and laughed while people watching at the party. We exchanged phone numbers long before the evening ended. That next weekend, we rendezvoused with some other gyrls from that same party. Introductions were made, and a good time was had. By our fourth outing, Sasha was calling me her "best friend." Now, gyrls, at the time, I could count my "best friends" on one hand . . . and three of those women were family. But (shoulder shrug) if Sasha wanted to label me a best friend, that was fine by me. What did it hurt?

Well, Gyrlfriends, I will tell you. Much like in romantic relationships, labels provide expectations and boundaries. For me, not every friend is a "best friend." How do you become a best friend? Well, there is no application process for that title. Best friends are created either through time and experiences or by a naturally existing counterpoint. I have many friends that I have known for many years, but the associations are not sufficient to win the label of best friend.

This is true for me because the title "best friend" carries responsibilities. As a "best friend," you might be called upon during times when no one else is expected to be present, and what's more, you might be expected to recognize those times without being told. "Best friend" is a label that creates an expectation of presence. The presence does not have to be physical.

My best friends and I are rarely in contact every day. In many cases, I go months and sometimes years without directly speaking to them. For a best friend, frequency and proximity are unimportant, but presence is critical. Best friends know when to show up and how to show up, and they do it because of what you mean to them, not because they are seeking acknowledgement or because it is what is expected. A "best friend" is more than a drinking buddy, a shopping sister, a party pal, or a tagalong. He[3] or she is more than someone you enjoy spending time with.

My best friends know me intimately, and not just because of the information I readily give up. Either through time or vulnerability, they have come to not only know my personality but are able to discern my spirit, and I am able to do the same with them. We encourage each other,

---

[3] Yes, females can have platonic male best friends. But this relationship is unique and, I would argue, usually starts in childhood.

we play hard, we call each other on bullsh*t, we lovingly speak harsh truths and are there to pick up the pieces after the fall out from those truths. "Best friends" are there even when *there* isn't fun. So, in all actuality, allowing Sasha to label me her "best friend" after having known me for only twenty-eight days caused a lot of damage. In hindsight, it may be the single reason for our tragedy.

You may have thought that this was to be the juicy story of how Sasha and I spiraled to the tragic end of our would-be sisterhood. It is not. This is the story of how I have come to realize that just because *you* may be whole in a situation doesn't mean that those attached to you are complete. I failed Sasha in many ways, but my biggest failure was my silence. Just like in many romantic relationships, my failure to communicate my needs and intentions, or my inability to recognize Sasha's needs and hurts, resulted in me walking away and her remaining stuck in the place of hurt and anger that I unknowingly found her in.

When I met Sasha, I was a whole person. I don't say this as a bragging point. I don't mean that I was better than her or more put together than her. When I say, "I was whole," I am stating that I was not suffering any lifetime traumas.

I come from a reasonably privileged background. My childhood and teenage years were sheltered, and I grew up with the full love and support of my parents, siblings, and extended family. I am—for the most part—secure in my position as Ariel. I have never had to question the love of my family or experience the kind of abuse or mistreatment that leaves holes in your heart and spirit.

I don't know all of Sasha's personal traumas, but as I got to know the sides of her that she revealed, it was evident that she had been broken and pieced back together. She was looking for "best friends" to provide the support for those pieces. She used attention, gathered through a multitude of "friendships," as the glue that kept her pieces in place. She created these friendships through apparent loyalty. She was always ready to show up. She was always willing to go the extra mile. She was always available to you, in the hopes that you would acknowledge her sacrifice and perhaps return the favor.

Let me be clear, I considered this woman to be a friend, perhaps even a good friend at one point. But I did not consider her to be a "best friend," and I believe this is where our relationship suffered. We were not equally yoked. I was always willing to show up. I would be available and do kind things. But the motivation behind my actions was not for the validation of my person. If I showed up, it was simply because I felt like being bothered. If I did a kind thing, it was because I felt like being kind. I did not need acknowledgment for the action.

Sasha relied on her friends in ways that I was not conscious of, or in ways that I did not acknowledge—not because I was inconsiderate or uncaring but because I wasn't looking to her for that kind of support. Because I was not seeking that deep level of support from her, I didn't recognize when she was requesting it from me. With my friendship, it was more egregious because, in her mind, I was one of *her* "best friends." This means that she expected all of the responsibility, insight, discernment, and presence that I spoke of earlier from me. *I*, was oblivious. But I did notice a few things, and as I transitioned out of my Rock-Star Lifestyle, those things began to grate my patience.

Sasha was needy. I don't mean bug-a-boo needy; I mean in need of constant validation needy. Sasha needed to be the center or near center of attention in most situations. She strived to be friends with everyone, no matter how brief their foray into the larger circle of friends. If she was not the focus, she needed to be credited for whoever had the focus. She was constantly at war with somebody, anybody. If she was in a disagreement with a mutual friend, she expected everyone to shun that person. She would campaign for their exclusion, creating unnecessary drama and strife. If an event or party was in full swing, and she felt that someone from whom she desired attention was not forthcoming, some sort of outburst would ensue. Crying, temper tantrums, fights, dancing like a wind-up toy in the middle of a laid-back party, whatever it took to capture her audience and receive the attention (the glue) she craved.

This was not a problem for me when we first met, remember, I was in it for the fun. A little drama makes for an interesting next-day story. In the beginning, Sasha's behavior was often a source of comedy or conversation. Everyone in the circle dismissed the behavior, myself included. "That's just Sasha."

179

Our friendship began to crack once I was out of school and evolving out of my Second Childhood. Once I was content to be at home watching *Scandal* on Hulu, and no longer seeking a partner-n-crime to run the streets, fissures began to develop. I believe this is when the trouble started because this is when I stopped actively looking for her. My calls to go places became less frequent because I was calm and happy in my own space, minding my own business. I would appear if called, but if no one called, I was at home with my boo or curled up with a giant coloring book watching tv.[4]

During this time, it was common for Sasha and me to be in fights that lasted for weeks, and that I knew nothing about. Seriously. Other people would have to call me and inform me that Sasha was upset with me. I wouldn't know because I hadn't talked to her. I would be assuming we hadn't talked because we were both living our lives. So not the case. We hadn't talked because she wasn't talking to me. She wasn't talking to me because I didn't call, or come over, or, I don't know. Unequally yoked.

I didn't need to be in constant contact with people to know that they cared about me. I believe she did (I could be totally wrong); so when I didn't check up, or stop by, it was as if I didn't care. This was complicated by the fact that she never told me that my apparent lack of

---

[4] I really do enjoy doodling and coloring. It is extremely relaxing, and I highly recommend it. I am not fond of "adult" coloring books. They tend to stress me out—all those tiny lines. My favorite is a giant Tinker-Bell book.

concern hurt her. By the time I would find out, I'd be so irritated by the situation, I would have little empathy or care for how she had come to her feelings.

These fissures soon turned into outright chasms. There were multiple incidents over the next two years that caused me to look at our relationship sideways. The term "toxic" kept coming to mind. Our relationship became a source of tension for me. I loved her, but she vexed me. There was always something wrong, always a disagreement or a disconnection. I would occasionally attempt to bridge the gap, but with no real effort because at the end of the day, I didn't care to spend the energy. In 2014, I suffered the penultimate upset at Sasha's hand.[5]

In 2014, my great-aunt passed away suddenly. She was the heartbeat of our family, and her death was like a sinkhole: unexpected and devastating. I was in a state of shock but felt the enormous responsibility of holding myself together so that my younger siblings and my mother had the space to fall apart. I remember thinking, "We can't all lose it. Somebody has to hold it together." All of my friends rallied as my aunt had touched everyone I associated with. A few of my friends truly stepped up in ways I did not require or expect.

---

[5] The Ultimate Upset and the event that truly broke our relationship happened later that year. There is no need to get into the details, just know that there was more than the incident discussed here.

Sasha was very kind. The day of the funeral, she stopped by my house and dropped off some deserts for my family because she wasn't able to attend the service. I was truly touched and told her thank you. After the service, I was exhausted. To avoid having to respond to a million text messages, I got on Facebook and genuinely thanked all of my friends for the support they had given my family. The members of my squad that had gone above and beyond all expectations of what a "friend" is required to do when someone's family member passes were called by name in the social media thank you.[6]

Sasha was not called by name. The next morning, not even 24 hours after the funeral service, I woke to a six-page text message condemning my friendship because I didn't mention her name in my general thank you. I cannot even explain the levels of "Bish, are you serious?!?!" that went off in my head that morning. I was utterly floored that she had found a way to make my aunt's death about her!! I did not respond to the text messages. In all honesty, I wanted to block her number. I could go into the reasons why those who were specifically named were singled out, but it doesn't matter. I now understand why Sasha's feelings were so hurt.

I don't think that Sasha consciously did things for recognition, but in her heart, that is what she was seeking. I believe when she dropped the sweets off that morning, it was because she was trying to do

---

[6] I could absolutely write an entire chapter about relying on social media to validate your relationships. DON'T DO THAT.

something nice, but the fact that I took time to acknowledge others and left her out cut her deeply. She couldn't see that the others were specifically mentioned because they had done extraordinary things. All she saw was the fact that her "best friend" didn't think anything of the time and effort she had placed in showing love. I, not desiring acknowledgment or validation,[7] rarely experience that kind of trauma at the hands of my gyrlfriends—so I couldn't see the damage that I had done in allowing her to place the label of best -friend on me.

I get it now. Our friendship cracked and shattered like Humpty Dumpty when she fell off that wall,[8] which actually makes a great discussion point. Why was Humpty Dumpty on the wall in the first place if she knew she was fragile and capable of shattering? Did she imagine that she was stronger than she really was, or did she believe she had friends in the King's Men? Did Humpty actually fall, or did she jump?! Did she throw herself from the wall to get the attention of the King's Men she believed to be her tribe? Did she perhaps think that the King's Men truly cared about her well-being enough to actually try to save her when she fell? And if they were her friends, why in the hell didn't the King's Men tell Humpty she shouldn't be up on the wall? Whether she tripped and fell, or threw herself from the battlements, Humpty had to know that playing up on the wall was bound to lead to her being open-

---

[7] I have my mom, sisters, cousins, and a boyfriend who provide that validation in my life.

[8] For the sake of our conversation, Humpty Dumpty shall be a gyrl. We can do that. It's a nursery rhyme, not history. For that matter, let us pretend that "the King's Men" is a sorority of women too.

faced on the street below. Upon Humpty's great tumble and impact, did the King's Men give her repair their best effort, or was the damage so severe that they merely looked at the mess, rearranged a few pieces, and gave it up as a bad job? Poor Humpty, lying there with her yolk and insides all over the concrete, waiting for somebody to give a damn. Is the lesson in Humpty's tale not to play on the wall, or to get better friends? . . . I'll just leave that there for us to contemplate together.

My point is that labels are important. They provide guidelines into how we should govern ourselves. They are not just important in romantic relationships but in our sisterhoods as well. If you are a person who instantly wants to call people you have a connection with a "best friend," I would challenge you to check yourself.

Ask yourself what that person has done to earn such a coveted space in your heart. Ask yourself whether you think that person is truly there for your needs, your hurts, your successes, and other aspects of your journey. Ask yourself how much you really know about that person. Do they confide in you? Do they actually listen when you talk? Do they even allow you to talk when you call or see them? If you do not have the answers to these questions, or if the answer to these questions is "no," perhaps you should allow that gyrl to just be a friend for a while, maybe not even a friend—maybe an associate.

On the flip side, if you are someone on the receiving end of an Instant Bestie situation, I challenge you to speak up. Be honest with that gyrlfriend. Explain to her that best friends have responsibilities and expectations, and that they must be cultivated over time and experience. There is nothing wrong with being honest about what type of friend you can be to someone. This is especially important if you know, or become aware, that the other gyrl may have been pieced back together in the past. Allow me to also say that we can absolutely develop new best friends as grown women, but it shouldn't be in the same manner you collected besties in middle school (you both have the same Lisa Frank folder, and now you're permanently attached at the hip . . . life as we get older typically isn't that simple). If you are like me, you are walking around wondering why you can't find your version of Carrie, Miranda, Charlotte, and Sam.[9] Tribes can be difficult to establish and maintain as adults. But just like the gyrlfriends on *Sex and the City* (or *Girlfriends*), those women came to that level of relationship over time and experience. They didn't run into each other and become that close overnight. We are grown. It takes some time and effort.

Being a good gyrlfriend means not allowing further harm to come to your gyrls, especially by your hand. My relationship with Sasha is over. She shattered our friendship because I continued to not be present for her, to not show up the way a best friend is supposed to show up. The sad part is that I did not realize the part I played in the tragedy of our relationship until I sat down to write this chapter. Hopefully, my

---

[9] Or Joan, Maya, Lynn, and Toni--if you didn't watch Sex and the City, but did watch Girlfriends.

soul searching and self-reflection can save another Humpty Dumpty from being splattered unnecessarily all over the concrete.

Meet The Authors

Dr. Marquita S. Blades

Serving as Chief Strategy and Innovation Officer, Dr. Blades is the co-founder of Gyrlfriend Collective, along with Maureen Carnakie-Baker and Cynthia A. Fontan. Together, Dr. Blades and her partners are working to build a movement that strengthens gyrlfriend connections using real-life stories being shared by real women from all walks of life.

Dr. Marquita S. Blades is an award-winning educator, international speaker, best-selling author, publisher, and education consultant with 16 years of experience as a high school science teacher and manager of national STEM programs for high-achieving high school students. Dr. Blades is the owner of Dr. Blades Consulting, which offers prescriptive solutions to learning institutions and individuals through professional development programs, curriculum & assessment writing, conference planning & programming, and individual teacher/education consultant coaching services in the areas of STEM Instruction and Teacher Burnout.

Dr. Blades is also the founder of The Mediocre Teacher Project© which helps teachers avoid and battle through burnout by incorporating their unique gifts and talents into their daily practice. In 2017, Dr. Blades launched The Dr. Marquita Blades Show-Candid

Conversations that Create Change, an internet-based broadcast dedicated to discussing current trends and issues in education. Dr. Blades is a contributing author for The Whole Truth & Lessons From My Grandmother's Lap – both anthologies. She is the lead author of The Mediocre Teacher Project and Chronicles of the Chronically Ill – also anthologies, and the author of POWARRful Teaching Strategies for Increasing Engagement & Collaboration While Maintaining Rigor in Science Courses – a collective of highly-effective instructional strategies for middle and high school science teachers.

Dr. Blades holds a Bachelor of Interdisciplinary Studies in Broad Field Science from Georgia State University, a Master of Science in Technical and Professional Communication from Southern Polytechnic State University, and a Doctor of Education in Instructional Leadership from Nova Southeastern University. When she is not working, Dr. Blades enjoys reading, cooking, and traveling with her husband. Learn more about Dr. Blades and her work by visiting www.drmarquitablades.com.

Laura Rudacille

Laura Rudacille is an author, premier member of the Women's Speakers Association, and creator of Awakening Goddess Retreats (AGR). Thirty years in the salon industry taught Laura the value of good listening and human connection. As women shared their experiences navigating the highs and lows of everyday life a root of commonality was exposed. Inspired, Laura published her novel Invisible Woman and expanded her vision to include workshops and destination retreats uniting and encouraging women to Connect on Purpose with Purpose. Her thought-partnering insight and candid humor sheds light on our similarities and infuses positivity and possibility into every moment. Discover more at www.LauraRudacille.com and join the conversation live on Facebook Sunday evenings in her private group for women's enrichment the AGR Hen House.

Nancy Mathieu

Nancy Mathieu makes her literary debut in The Gyrlfriend Code™ Volume 1 where she discusses secrets and what happens when trust is broken. Nancy received her Master's degree in Business Administration from Long Island University and has worked in the telecommunications industry for over twenty years. Nancy is using her experience from her friendship of twenty-five years with one of her best friends to join other authors in collaborating on The Gyrlfriend Code™. Nancy has an extreme passion for baking and cooking. Nancy lives in Long Island, NY with her family. To date, Nancy's greatest accomplishment is being the mom to her twin boys, which fills her heart with joy.

Ethlyn Elizabeth Lewis

Ethlyn Elizabeth Lewis, also known as, Lizzy has more than twenty years working in the legal field as a project management professional providing consultation, resolving disputes related to Department of Justice litigation cases, and preparing and producing documentation for Electronic Storage Information. While maintaining a long successful professional standing in this demanding industry, Lizzy has been journaling her life experiences. Now after thirty years she has built up the courage to share her testimony as a debut author in The Gyrlfriend Code ™. Lizzy was inspired to join the Gyrlfriend Collective and publish her very personal story by her twenty-four-year-old daughter, Tene' C. Lewis. Tene' is a graduate of St. John's University with a degree in Journalism and Photography. Lizzy and her daughter share a love for the written word and together they celebrate their accomplishments and are encouraging other women to cease all opportunities when they are presented. Lizzy attributes her survival to God. One of her favorite bible verses' is, "Trust in the Lord with all thine heart; and lean not unto thine own understanding. In all thy ways acknowledge him, and he shall direct thy paths (Proverbs 3: 5-6, King James Version)." Her favorite quote is, "It is never too late to be who you might have been" by George Eliot. Lizzy is peeling back the layers of her life experiences, good and bad, to let women know there is support out there. In her chapter, I Am My Sisters Keeper, she shows us how we can honor our sisterhood and strengthen our gyrlfriend bonds with a sip of support, a taste of love, and quench of encouragement, one glass at a time.

Cynthia A. Fontan

As Chief Branding and Engagement Officer and the co-founder of Gyrlfriend Collective, Cynthia A. Fontan, affectionately known as Cindy, is living her dream of becoming an agent for building strong connections among women who want to expand their network and support each other's personal growth. Together the dynamic trio of Cindy and Gyrlfriend Collective co-founders, Maureen Carnakie-Baker and Dr. Marquita S. Blades, are creating a movement that encourages women to share their experiences by publishing their most profound personal stories. In turn, the women involved in this movement are gaining self-confidence, acknowledging their self-worth, and inspiring others to accept who they are and become better versions of themselves. Cindy is a visionary author of The Gyrlfriend Code™ Volume 1 where she makes her literary debut as the author of the Honesty Code. In her chapter, Not Without My MasKara (spelled with a K), Cindy shares her personal story of battling high-functioning depression while hiding it from family and friends for decades.

With fifteen years in the healthcare industry, Cindy has managed professional relationships with government, and private entities focused on creating medical education content for clinicians. She has worked closely with high ranking academic publishers and collaborated with medical societies to develop educational materials. Currently, Cindy is a consultant in the medical education division of one of the world's largest drug manufacturing companies.

193

Cindy graduated from the Executive Master of Public Administration program at Bernard Baruch College School of Public Affairs in New York City. Then, she completed courses at the Fashion Institute of Technology in New York on color theory and style personality and became a Certified Image Consultant and Color Specialist through The Image Builder Academy.

As important as health and self-image are to her livelihood, Cindy underwent bariatric surgery in 2018. She is committed to getting healthy for herself, her family, and her career. Cindy will share her message of health and confidence in The Gyrlfriend Code™ Volume 2.

Follow Cindy on her journey while enjoying all things fashion, food, and friendship on Instagram @ohsochicvsglife or connect on LinkedIn at www.linkedin.com/in/cynthiafontan.

Dawn Ortiz

Dawn Ortiz, is a mother, daughter, sister, and aunt. She earned her degrees in psychology and community health at York College while raising her three daughters and working a full-time job. With a conviction and desire to help those in need, she has worked in the healthcare field for over twenty years completing and serving a variety of roles. Currently overseeing the Trauma and Acute Care Department for Northwell Hospital, Dawn meets and touches many lives with her joyful personality and loving nature. Her wisdom and trust in God helped her through her toughest times.

Dawn recognizes how far she has grown as a black woman from Brooklyn, New York. It is not only her strength and independence that guides her, but her compassion and discernment which she hopes are traits her daughters will duplicate. As a debut author in The Gyrlfriend Code™ Volume 1, Dawn shares her story of living through and surviving infidelities within her own relationship. She tells us of her experiences and dares to share them as to inspire someone on their journey to become resilient and stronger with time.

Dr. Melissa Noland Chester

Dr. Melissa Noland Chester is a former professor who taught on the collegiate level for approximately fifteen years. She is also the co-founder & CEO of the national nonprofit, Black Educators Rock, Inc. Dr. Noland Chester is committed to serving and impacting the lives of others by improving the situations of others through consulting, facilitation, and motivational speaking. Her dedication and passion for assisting individuals and organizations is evident in the many seminars, workshops, and programs she has participated in and implemented. Dr. Noland Chester is also a licensed real estate instructor and realtor for the state of Florida.

Dr. Noland Chester is married to Dr. Albert Chester II, and they have two sons, Aiden and Alexander.

You can visit her website at www.solutiontosuccess.com

Maureen Carnakie-Baker

Serving as Chief Contractual and Fiscal Officer, Maureen Carnakie-Baker, affectionately known as "Mo" is the co-founder of Gyrlfriend Collective, along with Dr. Marquita S. Blades and Cynthia A. Fontan. Maureen is a staunch advocate for financial health and wellbeing. Using her innate ability to connect with others, she works in the financial and healthcare technology industry as a consultant, providing advisory services to Fortune 500 companies.

Earning a Master's Degree in Social Work from the State University of New York at Stony Brook, and a Master's Degree in Business Administration from Georgia State University, Maureen is able to connect her love for people with her passion for fiscal health. After her contributions on how to handle financial situations with gyrlfriends, Maureen is using her financial acumen to publish a standalone resource to inspire and support the average nine-to-fiver.

From humble beginnings herself, she was one of five children born and raised in New York City. A middle child in a house full of predominantly women, life could be fun at times, and easily hormonal at others. Weekdays consisted of battles over bathroom time, while weekends entailed enjoying the latest jams from the radio while playing cards or dancing in the middle of the living room.

Known to many as the mediator, Maureen enjoys hanging with her grown babies, her gyrlfriends, hosting dinner parties, and lending a listening ear while strategizing on how to help you to solve your problem.

To this day, Maureen considers herself to be a quintessential student, labeling her journey, an eve-olution. She works diligently to keep up with an ever-changing financial and technological industry while helping others fill in the gap on their road to financial health.

A firm believer of incremental changes having the potential to yield substantial results, Maureen mentors others (youth and adults) aiming to cultivate untapped capability. Maureen knows that the right combination of knowledge, access, and confidence has the potential to be a generational game changer in the lives of others.

To take a peek at her inner-most thoughts, feel free to visit her anytime at: www.fortunetellher.com
Facebook: Fortune Tell Her
LinkedIn: http://www.linkedin.com/in/carnakiebaker

Favorite Quote by Warren Buffett
"It is not necessary to do extraordinary things to get extraordinary results."

Dr. Tricialand Hilliard

Dr. Tricialand Hilliard, affectionately known as Dr. T, is a licensed professional counselor, transformational speaker, visionary poet, and self-care advocate. Her work was featured in a documentary, *Black Women and Self-Care* by Christin Smith. Dr. Hilliard completed her research manuscript titled, *Understanding Counselor Wellness: an African American female counselor's burnout and cultural self-care preferences.* Her research aligned with eighteen years of clinical experience that focused on the wellness of black and brown women.

Dr. Hilliard recently traveled to Costa Rica and West Africa where she was inspired to focus her attention on self-care. Both experiences forged a personal spiritual journey which led her to launch the Self-Care Project. Her purpose is to help women take steps that will lead them to "S.H.I.F.T" (self-healing in focused treatment) and destigmatize the negative perception of mental health to a positive practice of mental wellness and self-care for black and brown women. In addition to the Self-Care Project, Dr. Hilliard is organizing the first wellness retreat conference titled, Living to Thrive Not Survive, in 2019.

Dr. Hilliard is a licensed professional counselor and founder & co-CEO of Pearls Noir Counseling and Consultations, LLC and operates two social media platforms, Black Self-Care Rocks and Black Wellness

Rocks, focused on creating a tribe of professionals who value their wellness, time, boundaries, space, and self-expression.

Dr. Hilliard is known to have coined the phrases "Dare to Self-Care" and "Words of Wellness."

If you have questions and want to connect with Dr. Hilliard, send an email to: selfcareandwellnessLLC@gmail.com.

Teresa Suber Goodman

A native of Clinton, SC Teresa Goodman is an author, mentor, and advocate for children's health and development. She is a fantasy football league commissioner and champion as well as a lifelong Pittsburgh Steeler fan. Her greatest joy comes from being the wife of Derrick and the mother of Xavier.

Throughout her career, Teresa has worked for various social service and nonprofit agencies. Currently, she is the Executive Director of Community Initiatives, Inc. where she directs multiple health and wellness programs for youth, adults, and seniors in a six-county area.

Goodman believes in community service and currently serves on the board of directors for the Bowers Rodgers Children's Home and The United Way of Greenwood & Abbeville Counties. She is the president of the United Way Partnership Council. A member of the Greenwood Alumnae Chapter of Delta Sigma Theta Sorority, Inc., Goodman is the chair of the fundraising committee and completed the South Atlantic Region's Leadership Fellows program. She is a graduate of the Greenwood County Chamber of Commerce's Leadership Greenwood program and was selected as a 2016 Connect Young Professional's Greenwood Under 40 Stars. As a member of The Women's Leadership Council, Teresa was chosen to co-chair the 2017 Women's Leadership Upstate Conference.

Teresa's life's motto is "Be the change you wish to see in this world."

Visit Teresa at http://Linkedin.com/in/teresa-goodman-b3934a22

E. Che'meen Johnson

E. Che'meen Johnson was born and raised in Brooklyn, New York. She is a third-generation homegrown property owner. For the past fifteen years, E. Che'meen has held both Residential and Commercial Property Management positions throughout New York City's five boroughs. Real Estate allows E. Che'meen the opportunity to provide direct service to individuals, families, and business by providing comfortable places for people to be; think and grow. She graduated from Marymount College, Tarrytown with a Bachelor of Science in Business Administration. E. Che'meen is the proud mother of a sixteen-year-old son, CJ and a cat named Sandwich.

Gyrlfriend Code, Vol. 1 is E. Che'meen's seventh published co-author contribution, the first being Tavis Smiley's 2002 book *Keeping the Faith*. Followed by 2015's *Fabulous New Life, Vol. 1* and 2016's *Women On A Mission, Sisterhood of Stories*. 2017 was an amazing year for E. Che'meen with her fourth, fifth and sixth co-authorships in *A Letter to My Abuser: Once a Victim, Forever Victorious; His Grace is Sufficient: He Turned My Mess into A Message* and *You Need It, I Got It: Conversations With Global Entrepreneurs On Growing Your Audience, Visibility and Influence*. E. Che'meen's first love has always been writing. Co-authoring seven anthologies has allowed E. Che'meen to express her writing voice on a range of topics and hone her writing skills.

E. Che'meen Johnson is all about polishing the diamond that she is. She is an outspoken, adventurous spirit with a flair for the dramatic. She is always open to the wondrous possibilities that life has to offer. Her fiery tenacity in approaching new experiences keeps her growing, developing and seeking her life's purpose. Her many outlets of expressions are writing, reading, coloring, dance classes, relaxing at the spa and traveling the world. Presently, she is working as the visionary author of her own anthology and has several non-fiction and fiction projects in the works. She is also building her public speaking portfolio.

Get to know E. Che'meen up close and personal at Echemeen.com.

Facebook: E Che'meen Johnson

Facebook Fan Page: Tell It Like It T'is

Instagram: echemeen

Twitter: echemeen

Ashley Little

Ashley Little is an entrepreneur and best-selling author of, *Dear Fear, Volume 2, 18 Powerful Lessons of Living Your Best Life Outside of Fear*. She is a co-host of The Tamie Collins Markee Radio Show and has been a guest on numerous podcasts, television shows, magazines, and radio shows. She is a strong leader who has a passion for changing lives through education and has worked in the for-profit education field for over 13 years holding several leadership positions. She is committed to helping students who may not have the opportunity to attend a four-year college to strive for success through other options.

In addition to being an author and innovator of education, Ashley is a Woman Speak Circle Leader and business owner. Through speaking engagements and workshops she teaches women skills to build their confidence, focus on emotional and mental health, and forge spiritual growth. Her message encourages women to speak up and break out of fear and to share their experiences with others as a way to grow their leadership skills.

Ashley is a proud member of Delta Sigma Theta Sorority Incorporated and Alpha Phi Omega. She is very involved in her community, social organizations, and non-profits. She is the co-founder of Sweetheart Scholars, a non-profit organization which provides financial scholarships to young aspiring African American females for college expenses. She believes in giving back to her community and is committed to providing direction and strong mentorships.

Ashley received her undergraduate degree in English from North Carolina A&T State University. She received her Master's Degree in Industrial-Organizational Psychology. She gives GOD all the credit for everything that has happened in her life. Her favorite scripture is Philippians 4:13 that says, "I can do all things through Christ who strengthens me."

Brittaney Pleasant

Brittaney Pleasant, also known as The Love Doula, is a wife, mother of four, nurse, relationship coach and birth doula. She is the author of *Break Every Chain: Powerful Prayers to Cover Your Husband.* Brittaney is a survivor of domestic violence and a domestic violence advocate. She is passionate about serving women in her community by helping them to understand the importance of self-love and fostering healthy relationships. Brittaney also has a passion for God and sharing His love with everyone she comes in contact with because she understands how it feels to experience His love when we have forgotten to how to love ourselves. She hopes to continue to be a source of inspiration and a glimpse of the heart of God to everyone she meets. You can connect with her at www.thelovedoula.com.

Ariel V. Dixon

Ariel V. Dixon is an artist, photographer, attorney, and small business owner. A creative at heart, when she is not engaged in the practice of law, Ariel enjoys a host of creative activities that include dancing, reading, photography, and painting. She is the owner of Doodles Paint & Geaux, LLC, a mobile painting party business located in Baton Rouge, Louisiana, providing a creative outlet for adults and children. She enjoys traveling with family and friends and is currently developing a program that combines her art and love of travel with her desire to assist in the empowerment of women of color to be their best selves.

Ariel graduated from Georgia State University with a degree in Political Science and earned a Juris Doctorate from the Southern University Law Center.

Visit Doodles Paint & Geaux at www.doodlespaingeaux.com and find Ariel on social media at @rel_vontreese and @geauxdoodles (Instagram and Facebook).

Made in the USA
Middletown, DE
16 January 2019